Principles of Design in Architecture

To build to suit some individual taste is an enforcement of the principle of vitality in Art.

Art is not fully appreciated unless it is true to contemporaneous Life.

Not that we should ignore the claims of posterity, but we should seek to enjoy and enrich the present more.

Nor should we disregard the creations of the Past but we should try to digest and assimilate them into our consciousness.

Slavish conformity to traditions and formulas fetters the expression of individuality and so of vitality in Archecture. We can only weep over those senseless imitations of European buildings which one beholds in progressive foreign nations. We marvel why Architecture should be so devoid of orginality, so replete with repetitious obsolete styles. Perhaps we are now passing through an age of the Democratization of Art, while awaiting the rise of some princely master who shall establish a new dynasty.

—Okakura Kakuzo, *The Book of Tea*, 1925

Principles of Design in Architecture

K. W. Smithies
Senior Lecturer
School of Architecture and Building Engineering
University of Bath

with drawings by
Steve Tompkins

VAN NOSTRAND REINHOLD COMPANY
New York – Cincinnati – Toronto – London – Melbourne

**Published by Van Nostrand Reinhold Company Ltd.,
Molly Millars Lane, Wokingham, Berkshire, England**

*Published in 1981 by Van Nostrand Reinhold Company,
135 West 50th Street, New York, NY 10020, USA*

*Van Nostrand Reinhold Limited,
1410 Birchmount Road, Scarborough, Ontario, M1P 2E7,
Canada*

*Van Nostrand Reinhold Australia Pty. Limited,
17 Queen Street, Mitcham, Victoria 3132, Australia*

Library of Congress Cataloging in Publication Data

Smithies, K. W.
    Principles of design in architecture.

    Bibliography: p.
    Includes index.
    1. Architectural design. I. Tompkins, Steve.
II. Title.
NA2750.S58   729   81-2278
ISBN 0-442-30441-2   AACR2
ISBN 0-442-30442-0 (pbk.)

Printed in Great Britain at
The Camelot Press Ltd, Southampton

I wish to acknowledge Miss Lesley J. Ward, Managing Editor at Van Nostrand Reinhold, for her encouragement in undertaking the work at the start and for her patience in awaiting the result at the end.

Contents

1
Introduction

When discussing this topic with my teaching colleagues I have been asked about the sources of the theory and the basis of the assumptions about our expectations in design. The primary, and major, influence was provided by Professor Lionel Budden who, when requested by a number of students returning to the Liverpool School in 1946, agreed to talk to us about the bases of architecture. His lectures gave me the essence of earlier theories including the Beaux Arts influence on education. While these theories were related to past, stylistic, examples I found that the method of analysis could be applied to our current problems, with some small modifications. When asked for advice by students of junior years it seemed that they were helped by the use of a 'framework' of objectives. This was my first interest in teaching which was to reassert itself after some years in practice.

My early years of teaching were with part time students who were preparing 'Testimonies of Study' for a part of their qualifying examination while working full time in offices. Although many of these students had considerable experience in practical matters they still had great difficulty in dealing with design problems. In many cases it was their experience in practice which was the impediment in their thinking. It was here that I found that the students needed a framework of objectives in order to correct the imbalance in their priorities. During some 25 years of working with students the Principles have evolved and changed. They have proved particularly useful in determining which group of intentions or expectations is being considered at any one time and in relating the importance of one group to another. The students themselves have played a considerable part in the assessment of our expectations of a design, particularly the visual aspects.

My thinking about thinking has also been influenced by students and by many of my colleagues in teaching and in practice. The most stimulating influence in that area of activity has been provided by Karl R. Popper. I would like to quote from a passage in his *Objective Knowledge: An Evolutionary Approach* (Published in 1972) which I believe is central to the problem of design in architecture.

'We start, I say, with a problem, a difficulty. It may be practical or theoretical. Whatever it may be when we first encounter the problem we cannot, obviously, know much about it. At best, we have only a vague idea what our problem really consists of. How, then, can we produce an adequate solution? Obviously we cannot. We must first get better acquainted with the problem, but how?

My answer is very simple: by producing an inadequate solution, and by criticising it. Only in this way can we come to understand the problem. For to understand a problem means to understand its difficulties; and to understand its difficulties means to understand why it is not easily soluble — why the more obvious solutions do not work. We must therefore produce more obvious solutions; and we must criticise them, in order to find out why they do not work. In this way we become acquainted with the problem, and may proceed from bad solutions to better ones — provided always that we have the creative ability to produce new guesses, and more new guesses.

This, I think, is what is meant by 'working on a problem'. And if we have worked on a problem long enough, and intensively enough, we begin to know it, to understand it, in the sense that we know what kind of guess or conjecture or hypothesis will not do at all, because it simply misses the point of the problem, and what kind of requirements would have to be met by any serious attempt to solve it. In other words, we begin to see the ramifications of the problem, its sub-problems, and its connection with other problems.'*

Other influences, through reading, are given at the end of the book. I would mention, in particular, Edward de Bono's *The Mechanism of Mind* (1969).

Because architecture represents a multiple problem, where the satisfaction of one group of objectives may conflict with the requirements of another, I have emphasised the use of Principles as a way of grasping the total problem and introduced the spiral to represent the manner of considering and inter-relating objectives. It also underlines the need for constant reiteration during the design process. Over the years I have found that students must be encouraged to establish their intentions and the priorities which they would allot as a preliminary to designing. Frequently a design will be unsatisfactory, not because of a student's inability to synthesise his objectives, but because his expectations were inadequate. This leads to the assumption that, when we criticise a solution, we may be asserting that the intentions were inappropriate so that there are two aspects of judgement; first, concerning the intentions held and, second, regarding the measure of success in synthesis. Constant reappraisal is a necessary part of the design process. The understanding of our own expectations can have a profound effect upon the outcome. In other words we are unlikely to satisfy design objectives not included in our original intentions or, more correctly, unless they are introduced at some stage. As we criticise our tentative solution we tend to change our intentions but we are unlikely to satisfy aspects which are completely absent from our expectations.

The spiral is, of course, an idealised representation of the way in which we pursue a solution: in fact the mind moves over the contents of the problem and the expectations we hold in an erratic manner. Ideas form intuitively but can be influenced by the way in which we order and assess the information gathered.

It would be misleading to suggest that a student of architecture can gain proficiency by reading alone. The long-held tradition in architecture of learning by doing is essential to the gaining of the required skills. The practice of architecture is a skill and like all skills requires much practice. Thus the single most important activity for the student of architecture is in studio work. I have always argued for the importance of the studio master; the way in which design exercises are set and supervised is crucial to the development of the student's skill and yet the year master must be fully aware of the problems of practice offices in which the student must, eventually, survive. For this reason the studio masters should have reasonable practical experience, but this does not mean that practical experience is superior to, or even a substitute for, the controlled design exercise. The priorities in practice tend to be distorted in favour of satisfying building controls, avoiding litigious mistakes and cost control. Not that any of these are unimportant, but the young student can be permanently disabled by being exposed to the priorities of today's hard pressed practitioner before he has been allowed to develop a more balanced understanding of the requirements of the art of architecture.

Another of Popper's theories describes three realms of being or activity. The second is that of the realm of action or the will to act and the third is that of ideas or theories. The architect must practice in a world of action, but he benefits from periods of dwelling among theories which he can take with him back to the world of action. Today the student of architecture needs a theoretical framework which is to last him for the remainder of his working life — some thirty to forty years — in which requirements and methods are liable to change many times.

Architecture is a difficult profession requiring a long and rigorous training which must equip the student to hold and maintain objectives in the face of such adverse pressures that, at times, he will be the only one to see the full range of appropriate expectations. To do so will require understanding but more than anything else he will need courage.

---

* Reproduced by permission of Oxford University Press.

2
Intentions

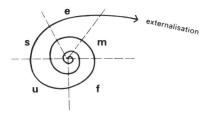

In recent years much of what has been written about architecture describes no more than the requirements of building.

If we accept that essential practical needs and the limits of construction affect building and architecture we may reasonably ask what constitutes architecture. What values must be observed in order to produce beauty?

In very simple terms our main appreciation of these values is through seeing. These visual qualities are not a mystery shared only by architects and a few of their confidants. Everyone responds to his or her surroundings. The response may not be a conscious one and it may not be pleasant but we are all affected by the setting in which we live and work. We can be stimulated by it, reassured, frightened or simply bored, but it will have a powerful and continuing effect. Architects can achieve pleasant visual designs by intuition. Indeed many theorists, having analysed the practical requirements common to building and architecture, dismiss the visual objectives as an entirely subjective area of design to be dealt with by the intuitive flair of the architect. It should not be assumed from this that a building can be designed to meet the practical requirements and then tinkered with to satisfy the visual objectives of architecture.

The architect — particularly the student of today — must develop a framework of 'intentions', a theory which enables him to seek the visual qualities of architecture simultaneously with his resolution of practical needs and means. He must be able to see the practical objectives always in the light of visual intentions as he strives to synthesise them all.

Many architects, with a strong intuitive sense of visual design, manage to combine all aspects of architecture in this way. When entry to the profession and training emphasised visual qualities through the influence of the Beaux Arts there was sufficient bias to ensure a proper regard for visual composition at least. The student today will need a more conscious awareness of visual intentions if he is to produce architecture within the limitations of building legislation. In his training the student of architecture needs to reinforce his visual awareness and his ability to control composition ahead of the pressures of practical necessity.

The evidence of our surroundings in Britain today and the public's attitude to recent developments are measures of the degree to which many buildings are not architecture. The disenchantment is such that all new buildings are held in suspicion and architects too; but all past periods of architecture were new in their time and there is reasonable evidence, although not in the majority, that modern architecture can be as visually satisfactory as anything which has gone before. Unfortunately, poor designs, even those which are positively ugly, mimic the modern idiom by using visual clichés taken from better work but used without regard for good composition or expression. The result is visually repulsive but is associated with modern architecture because of some similarities in appearance, like wearing clothes of similar material but ill arranged and shoddy. Of course we cannot pursue good visual design at the expense of function and stability: the architect must produce a sound and useful building. But equally we cannot excuse bad visual surroundings on the grounds of efficiency or economy. Architecture and beauty are achieved when all intentions are satisfied in one integrated whole.

Why has this situation arisen? In the past a new style was established by a few architects, artists or craftsmen. The style, once established, became the accepted mode of building and all past styles combined visual objectives with those of structure or purpose. In the course of time others modified and changed the development, but there was an overall continuation of the basic style with visual aspects being refined as much as practical matters. In other words, the work within a particular style modified and changed its course to meet new problems or to improve upon what had gone before, but the style and its evolution were closely integrated with visual and geometric order. Proportions and visual integrity were preserved because they were inherent in the style.

The pioneers of the modern movement in architecture were seeking a new basis of design not related to a single geometric or even a structural system. Nevertheless, the work of the pioneers indicated a concern for visual composition — not in the manner of a visual style, but rather as the satisfaction of fundamental principles. The work of Le Corbusier, Frank Lloyd Wright and Saarinen can be compared to show examples of good composition yet are completely unrelated to one another. While the pioneers and their more sensitive followers demonstrated their concern for visual intentions by their work, the majority of those who followed attempted to copy the appearance of the new work without really understanding their objectives or appreciating that the modern movement was not a visual style in the way of previous eras. Many followers lacked an understanding of composition and even the older treatises were of little use because the illustrations were 'out of date'.

The last 25 years has seen a decline in visual standards in architecture unprecedented in history. This lack of visual quality together with the overriding concern for economic expediency has brought us to the point where even Victorian buildings are preferred to those which replace them. Some Victoriana is pleasant and interesting, but much is coarse and falsely stylistic. That many contemporary buildings can be worse is the greatest condemnation of all.

Inevitably, this state of affairs has prompted more and more conservation of existing buildings. Insensitive design is being replaced by buildings which strive to fit in with the existing. Commendable as these pursuits may be it also indicates a lack of confidence when new work attempts to match the existing, without merit, and, even worse, 'mirror' faced buildings are used as though to reflect their — any — surroundings. What, one may ask, will be the effect when all are faced to reflect each other in ever receding planes of mirror glass?

I said before that the appreciation of architecture is not the prerogative of architects. It seems to me that the public, in questioning contemporary building, is applying, if only intuitively, basic visual standards which should be essential components of the architect's vocabulary. A vocabulary which was used in the past and, from the examples of the past, still influences the public today. If people say they like the work of the Elizabethan or Georgian periods it is not to say that they like only that period of design in that form. They are expressing a liking for the visual qualities they see in those works and find lacking today. An assertion in favour of the eternal verities should encourage us to find why they are lacking today, not to attempt to recreate past styles.

It is only in exceptional circumstances that we need or can afford to build today in imitation of the past. The modern movement provides no geometric idiom to guide the less able designer. The building which inspires the eclectic may be quite unsuited to his own task. The architect who follows fashion without basic design principles will be in danger of serious error. The student must appreciate and understand the good of the past and the present by the way in which they satisfy the design objectives appropriate to their time, place and purpose.

If architecture is to survive and evolve it must respond to the influences of new methods and materials, it must satisfy changing needs but, most important, it must meet our expectations for satisfactory visual surroundings.

The influences on architects today are enormous, the areas of expertise to be embraced are too much for one man to master. Nevertheless, the architect must integrate all objectives because even those things best devised by consultant experts are part of the total visual organisation. If aspects are ignored because they cannot be mastered the work will be the poorer. The architect must understand the way in which his design is to be used and this requires a wide understanding of human activities, and other needs as well. Equally the building must be sound and well suited to its purpose. For this he must understand structural engineering and be responsible for the detailed technical content of the building and its many services. These objectives are the ones we can call common to building and architecture. The resolution of these requirements produces visual characteristics which are subject to other, visual, objectives to be achieved and integrated in the process of ordering the total design solution.

All these objectives may vary in priority; because of the problem itself, because of the designers own inherent ability and shortcomings or because of external factors. The design which fails to meet essential practical requirements will fail as a building and as architecture. The designer who lacks the sensitivity or skill to achieve a visually satisfying solution may provide a serviceable building but it will not be architecture.

All aspects of design react one upon another so that all are interrelated. However, in working with students I find it helpful to consider the basic objectives as five principles of design.

Three of the principles relate to visual objectives: (1) the visual composition, that is the syntactical relationship of part to part and each part to the whole in visual terms; (2) the semantics, that is the effect of a design on the mind of the observer, or expressiveness; and (3) the wider relationship between design and setting in place and time, also its direct relationship to human size — magnitude.

Each principle, alone, is reasonably simple to understand. The difficulty, for the architect, is that he must try to satisfy all objectives without diminution of any. Thus, no solution is perfect, compromise is inevitable and one of the architect's most important tasks is to establish the right priorities at an early stage of the design process and be able to maintain them throughout the design process.

The ability to synthesise a solution from these objectives requires knowledge and skill, a skill which requires long practice.

The scientific way of establishing acceptable intentions in architecture might have been on the basis of evaluation of 'personal constructs', i.e. the collection of a wide range of individual likes and dislikes about architecture. The difficulty with this method is the problem of reconciling the many and varied descriptions by different people studying even a simple object. The principles of design have been applied in the teaching of students over many years and modified so as to cover every aspect of design, but in a way which — as far as possible — is intelligible and acceptable to the great majority of students. This is not to say that further change could not take place. As they stand the principles represent a set of 'constructs' which allow every aspect of design to be embraced although accepting that some are very subjective, some likely to have very different levels of impor-

tance or acceptance for different people. The principles therefore are not fixed objectives or rules. They represent a method of communication which allows us to consider a designer's intentions and his attempt to satisfy them.

Different designers may still give much greater importance to one principle or aspect than another. The important thing is that a relevant design objective is not ignored because there is no consideration given to it or because there is undue bias in the assessment of the student's work.

In order to produce architecture we must at least start with the right intentions if we are ever to gain the skill to achieve them.

3
Unity

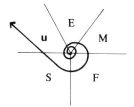

The principle of Unity is concerned with visual composition in design. Composition in this sense is produced by the relationship between the visual ELEMENTS. The brickwork, timber or concrete we use as building materials to keep out the weather or for structural support also provide the visual elements which form the composition. These occur in any building whether it is a good composition or not and it is important in our understanding of Unity that we can distinguish between the elements, which occur in any case, and the ASPECTS of Unity which we must attempt to satisfy if we are to produce a satisfactory composition.

Elements of Unity

Let us first consider the elements of composition. While we recognise materials as stone, glass or steel, what we see are a variety of colours, tones and textures. These are inherent aspects of most building materials, but it must be remembered that the texture or colour of say a single brick or panel will be different when it is seen en masse. Then, the brick and its joint, or the panel and its frame, becomes part of a larger texture.

Texture. This is not only the range from smooth to rough, but includes decoration and carving. In a large composition, or any design seen at a distance, larger elements, even individual dwellings within a group, can produce an effect of texture.

Colour. This can be analysed in detail by a study of such systems as the Munsell. For our present purpose we will refer simply to colour hue, but we must not forget, however, that there are secondary characteristics of colour such as luminance, fullness and transparency which can extend the possible variations in composition.

Tone. This is usually dealt with as part of colour theory. It is referred to as greyness in the Munsell system and describes the neutral scale of white to black through a range of greys. In design composition we will find it helpful to consider tone separately. It plays a very important part in architecture as well as in the drawings we use to represent buildings. If you half close your eyes and look about you or look at any drawing so as to heighten the distinction between different tones, it becomes quite evident how much we rely upon tonal variation both for the identification of what we see, and as an element of composition.

Direction. Every building has elements which suggest direction. In most buildings there are strong elements of vertical and horizontal direction given by the shape of the building as a whole, by its parts and by its structural components, its window and other openings. By studying building interiors or exteriors it is possible to assess the overall visual effect of the horizontals and verticals in their composition.

Proportion. In architecture, this is the geometric relationship of the sides of rectangles and volumes, also the ratio or comparison of different parts of the composition. We do not measure these relationships accurately by eye, but we can compare them and tend to judge the relationship of one part to another on a proportional basis. Classical and Gothic architecture, with its greater detail, contained many more and varied proportional relationships than most buildings today. The evidence of the buildings of the past, and such information on their design as has survived, all indicate a very high concern with proportional relationships. It might be thought that the simpler forms of modern buildings place less emphasis on proportion, but it could be argued that, with fewer elements, there is a need for even greater care in their arrangement.

School, England
This illustration shows a variety of textures (roofs, walls and paving), giving interest combined with a number of strongly identifiable shapes — forms — in the roofs which, related to the battered walls below, can be seen as repeating units.

Ducal palace, Urbino, Italy
Harmony through proportion. The classical ideal where each part is related to every other part and to the whole through related geometric proportions.

The City Theatre, Helsinki, Finland (Timo Penttilä)
Strong dominance of horizontality is given by the roof line and overhang with contrast from the columns. The directional emphasis is reinforced by the use of a strongly ribbed cladding tile which can be seen to run horizontally on the eaves soffit and the beams linking the column heads and vertically on the columns and the solid parts of the wall behind them.

Flats, Bremen (Aalto)
A dominantly vertical composition where the verticality is reinforced by the faceting of the envelope. Contrast is given by the generally horizontal emphasis of the fenestration.

The curving round of the plan in this way also affords more window space for the living accommodation on the southerly side relative to the service and circulation space on the north: stairs, lifts, passage access to flats.

Solid and Void. The apparent effect of solid and void is peculiar to architecture. It is produced by the relationship between solid material and the voids of windows or other openings and, internally, in the way in which spaces are formed by the arrangement of the solids which surround them. Although it embraces direction and proportion this relationship provides a distinctive element of composition.

Cemetery chapel, Turku, Finland (Bryggman)
The relationship between solid and void. The dominance of solid material contributes to the sense of enduring unity. The porch and opening above give some limited contrast, but the major source of vitality is the contrast between the building and the many natural elements of the setting.

Form or Shape. These may be seen in the overall arrangement of a building or in its parts where these have recognisable geometric shapes. Repetitions or variations of particular forms can provide a very strong element of composition. While shapes may contribute to proportion or direction, they do provide a separate characteristic arising from the way in which we are able to recognise distinctive forms. For instance, the pitch of a roof will provide a certain form which we will recognise quite easily and relate to other roofs which have a similar pitch. When a roof is of a distinctly different shape it will appear strongly dissimilar. Repetitions of gables or oriels may be seen as a series of matching shapes, even related shapes of different sizes.

These are the basic elements of composition. When we look at a building superficially we may not recognise them or distinguish between them. Nevertheless, we assess their overall effect and respond to what we see either intuitively or consciously. Many students can compose their designs intuitively to produce Unity, particularly when the practical constraints are simple. As a building becomes more complex we find it more and more necessary to identify the aspects of Unity in order to maintain good composition in the face of increasing technical complexity.

Aspects of Unity

The aspects of Unity contribute collectively to a satisfactory visual whole. They should not be seen as a check list, but rather as a number of inter-related requirements the importance of which is partly subject to individual preference and greatly influenced by other principles of design. The aspects of Unity are dominance or self unity, harmony, vitality and balance.

A simple object such as a sphere or an egg is an obvious visual entity having self-unity. Fishes and birds, like submarines and aircraft, are subject to aerodynamic and hydrodynamic forces which impose upon them a simplicity of form. This gives an effect of self-unity — at least at a distance. Simple buildings can produce a similar effect; an isolated crofter's cottage for instance. However, as we look more closely at an aircraft or a cottage, what appears simple at a distance is seen to contain a number of visual elements which arise from the detailed requirements of function and stability. So roofs, walls, windows and doors all provide colours, tones, textures, direction, solid to void, etc. As the visual elements increase, there is a greater tendency for competitions to arise. Thus we find a need for a visual dominant as a means of avoiding dualities or competitions of equal interest.

Dominance. This may be provided by the effect of one colour, tone or texture being visually stronger than the remainder. A dominance of direction would mean that the horizontals were stronger — collectively — than the verticals or, alternatively, that there is a dominance of verticality. A dominance of solid over void or vice versa is necessary to avoid an equal competition which would tend to destroy unity. A dominant form or shape can help to provide a sense of unity. Quite obviously, unity cannot exist if there is a duality or competition of visually equal elements. A student's early work is often preoccupied with simply avoiding dualities and pluralities. The difficulty, and one of the reasons why so much practice is necessary, is that while we are trying to overcome one visual weakness we frequently lead ourselves into producing others. For dominance is only one aspect of unity and, as we must constantly remember, our visual objectives must be achieved with due regard for the demands of other principles.

Harmony. This is the next aspect of unity. *Colour* harmony means what it says; colours being related by being near to each other in the colour wheel (or colour solid), that is to say colours which are associated with one hue, e.g. browns, golds and yellows all near to the yellow hue sector. Harmony of *texture* may mean simply a matching textural quality although, with the bolder textural effects of some materials, even carving, we can associate some textures, e.g. ribbing, as being related even when they are not identical. *Tones* can be harmonious only in the sense of being of equal tonal value. Some recent graphic art has employed colour change — contrast in combination with equal tones. In architecture there is usually a tendency to use a more harmonious colour range in combination with tonal contrast. There is no particular reason why this should be so, except that when there is little sunlight a lack of tonal change produces a rather dull sunless effect. Florentine palaces illustrate the use of one colour of the stone with textural contrasts given by the treatment of the stone (rusticated bases or strongly emphasised joints in some parts, with smooth ashlar in another). In this case, the tone may appear equal in dull lighting, but the strong Italian sunlight produces tonal changes through the shadows in the texture. It may be worth noting that when we use two materials together, e.g. brickwork and concrete, we are in fact introducing colour, textural and tonal changes simultaneously. If this is not appreciated in advance, and drawings may not always show this effect, we can find that we have produced multiple competitions of equal elements.

Harmony of *direction* at its simplest may mean simply the same direction. In a complex composition the directional forces arise from a number of materials and components, even the spaces or solids between them, and we must learn to measure and relate the directional effect produced by our

Chateau de Chambord, France
The string courses and fenestration of the three main floors give a strong horizontal emphasis reflecting the overall form of the building. Above these floors the roof provides a number of different contrasts: form, tone and colour. The repeating domed roof pinnacles, chimney groups and dormer-type windows give an impression of a busy cluster of visual elements arising from relatively simple functional/structural elements.

designs. The direction provided by the total building shape must be seen in relation to the elements within it. An equal effect of direction between the two will form a visual duality.

Proportion can be a powerful element in providing harmony of composition. This is particularly so in three-dimensional design. Much has been written on the subject of proportion in Greek architecture. The influence of Plato and the Pythagoreans is believed to have affected the architecture of Greece, although the philosophers were seeking a basis of universal or cosmic harmony. Greek design was strongly influenced by a concern for harmoniously modulated composition. The harmonic relationship of part to part and part to whole was based upon proportional systems, the best known being the golden section or divine proportion. This is $(\sqrt{5} + 1)/2$ or 1:1.618; this ratio provides a very wide choice of combinations. The negative value of $\frac{1}{2}(1 - \sqrt{5}) = -0.618$. The square of the value $1.618^2 = 2.618$ or $1.618 + 1$. The reciprocal $1/1.618. = 0.618$ so $2.618/1.618 = 1.618$. As a series $(0.618:1:1.618:1.618^2:1.618^3:1.618^n)$ it has the same property as a Fibonacci series (each number being the sum of the two numbers preceding), e.g. 2:4:6:10 etc. As a geometric progression it is analogous to the spiral curve of organic growth. Thus, the golden section ratio can act as the key proportion for the development of a whole series of related shapes. Any Fibonacci series quickly reaches the proportions of 1:1.618 and the property of producing similar growing surfaces and volumes by simple accumulation is why the Fibonacci series is important in botany.

However, although the subject of harmonic porportion is fascinating and capable of very detailed study, it is only part of one aspect of unity. Certainly it is possible to develop whole networks of proportional relationships as did Le Corbusier in his Modulor. The important point for architects is that this is concerned with proportion and should not be confused with modular co-ordination which is related to dimensions. In considering the principle of unity we should attempt, wherever possible, to see our designs in terms of proportion and consider harmonic relationships where appropriate and possible. The pressures of technical integration have forced architects to concentrate more upon dimensional co-ordination of details. Too often our concern for proportion has been eroded by such factors. If anything, proportional relationships are simpler than in the past and yet, paradoxically, have been given much less consideration. If nothing else is attempted it is worth analysing our designs in terms of proportion to study the extent to which shapes and spaces have been, or could be, related to one another. (This is easily done by setting a

The Hermitage, Assisi, Italy
The dominant element in this composition is provided by the mass of solid walling. Harmony is given by the use of one material in the walls, by the repetition of some of the small windows and the arched collonade at the rear.

Vitality is contributed by a variety of opening size and shape, the changes in shape and roof slope direction of the several parts of the building and the contrasting forms of the setting.

The rhythm and repetition of the heavy Roman roof tiles adds to the harmony and the vitality.

11

set square at the angle of say 31° 43' — the diagonal of the golden section — and checking a design to see if this proportion or its harmonics can be used to relate the parts of a building in plan, section and elevation.)

Repetitions of *forms* or *shapes* can be used to produce rhythms — a particularly useful way of providing harmony. However, any repetition taken too far without change, any colour tone or texture used without relief, will eventually tend to monotony. This, in turn, will destroy unity.

Russian church

The multiple repetition of the lower arch forms building up to a crescendo in the five domed pinnacles, the middle one being slightly higher, richer and crested, is an example of repetition of shapes contrasting with another group of shapes using distinctive and unifying forms with strong contrast of tone.

The importance of the composition is enhanced by enrichment, in the gilding of the domes and the decoration and piercing of the visual elements.

Olympic Stadium, Munich, Germany

The repetition of the triangular ends to the structural frame projecting beyond the facade sets up a strong rhythm. The response of the arched top infil panels enhances the repetition and gives contrast — of tone and material — as well.

The overall horizontality of the building is emphasised by the light and dark horizontal bands in the elevation: a light contrast is given by the vertical glazing bars at each level and the repeated twin beam ends at the lowest storey.

Vitality. This is given by interest and, in visual design, this aspect of unity is provided mainly, but not exclusively, by contrast.

Contrast of colour, tone or texture, of direction or proportion, between solid and void, can all give interest and vitality to a design. But just as harmony taken too far can lead to monotony, so too much contrast or too many contrasting elements will impair harmony and tend to produce a multiplicity of equal interests. This in turn reduces any dominance and weakens unity. Too blatant a contrast will tend to duality, the use of too many different elements leads to visual chaos.

Classical and Gothic architecture provide many examples of harmony and vitality combined to the benefit of both, in particular, the use of rhythms which contain contrasts, e.g. ABACAD rhythm of trygliphs and metopes of classical design or the repetition of columns with capitals constantly varied in Gothic churches. The combined discipline and extreme vitality of the royal portal at Chartres illustrates the use of order integrated with contrast in the relationship between the columns and the carved figures. Modern architecture tends to use bolder contrasts, and, while this must be expected with simple forms, there is often a tendency to blatant contrast which produces a striking initial interest, but one which quickly palls. The size and form of many larger buildings makes the element of direction of particular importance. Strong direction overall or

Cathedral, Pisa, Italy
Simple forms giving immense rhythm and change. Note the way in which the buttressing repeats throughout each floor but changes at each level, the ABAB rhythm of windows in the panels formed by the buttresses alternating with other decorative motifs. The bay widths at each floor change but are related visually. The stone itself gives a further interest through textural change. The roof texture and ridge finials give yet more. Bold, simple but vital.

Conference Centre, Berchtesgarten, Germany
The dominant element throughout this composition is horizontality. This is seen in the overall proportions of the building shape, the line of the roof, and the balconies — reinforced by the projecting balustrades — which give the feeling of floating horizontal planes and a number of smaller features.

Vitality from contrast of direction is produced by the vertical joints in the roof eaves cladding, the balustrade supports and the structural frame as it rises through the floors of the building. These vertical elements, as well as giving contrast of direction, set up a number of rhythms which, with the use of materials, help to give harmony.

Church, Leningrad, USSR
This illustrates a combination of repeated form — the domes — but differing in size and texture in the way the surface treatment of each dome is different. There are more contrasts in the repetitive arcuated drums to the domes as well as in the fenestration of the building below.

in 'banding' of the elevation is given vitality by the contrast in direction of smaller components. Care must be taken to avoid competitions of direction and one should clearly dominate.

Compared with many historic examples, some buildings today seek vitality at the expense of harmony. This is not to say that our designs should be dull, but we must remember that a building is in being much longer than it exists on our drawing boards. This means we should seek to provide more subtle interest. Nature provides the designer with many inspirations for the integration of harmony and vitality. We can find examples in any plant or shrub, any animal or bird and in any pastoral scene. Note how the various forms provide rhythms combined with tonal or colour harmony and contrast. This fusion of Unity with Function and Stability in Nature is of course the ideal design synthesis, something we may emulate but rarely equal.

Balance. The last aspect of Unity is balance. In architecture this is not usually a problem as the requirements for movement, under Function, and of structure, under Stability, lead us towards a balanced massing at least. Nevertheless, a design can be lacking in balance even though other aspects have been satisfied. Hence we must consider balance as a separate objective. It is seldom possible to correct a lack of balance in massing by minor adjustments in the composition, but usually requires some reconsideration of the whole design concept — if this is possible. Of course, we have to be able to appreciate a general view of a design to appreciate this aspect. In crowded urban sites it is sometimes difficult to provide a balanced massing and pointless, too, if it cannot be seen. Finer effects of balance can be given by the effective visual 'weight' of elements and the positions of solid and void.

So much for the essentials of Unity. For the student, it is merely a statement of a vocabulary of composition. Expertise will only develop with practice and that practice must include the integration of other principles.

The Search for Unity

It quickly becomes evident during the practice of design that the search for Unity is complicated by the enormous number of variations which can be introduced; even when there are few visual elements. It is more important, initially, to understand how the elements of composition occur and to develop a sense of appreciation for Unity as a whole. As this is done one is able to sense a lack of Unity and develop design skill partially by intuition, but assisted by repeated conscious analyses of composition to determine what is lacking.

It was Yehudi Menhuin who said something to the effect that music can be created — and appreciated — either intuitively or intellectually, but that, at their best, the two seemed to become the same. I believe this is to be true of architecture and particularly in the matter of Unity where intuition or conscious effort can lead to similar solutions.

I have found, for instance, that a student can be helped by encouraging him to seek a visual dominant at an early stage of designing. If we study the work of architects like Frank Lloyd Wright, Mies Van der Rohe or Saarinen it seems that they have provided a major dominant first and that everything flows from that decision; the house at Bear Run with its dominant horizontality and the IIT School of Architecture building with a dominance of direction and of void over solid. The provision of a strong visual dominant

House at Bear Run, Pennsylvania, USA (Frank Lloyd Wright)
This design is famous because of its imagination in the use of materials and the great sense of vitality it conveys. The bold, floating, horizontal canti-levers in the balconies contrast with the main vertical mass both in direction and texture. The whole sits into and yet contrasts with the beautiful natural setting and it is probably the delightful use of the stone, trees and water of the setting which gives such dramatic quality. There are also a number of minor rhythms and contrasts in the fenestration, steps and structural forms which add to the composition and provide a series of interests. (Reproduced from *Building Design*, 1980, by permission.)

allows the integration of the practical requirements without loss of unity because, while these produce contrasts, they remain subordinate to the dominant. Frank Lloyd Wright prairie houses are so strongly horizontal that all the necessary components merely produce interest without competition.

With a strong dominant, it is so much easier to provide harmony and vitality through the integration of the building components.

Harmony and vitality, we soon find, are two related aspects. While the ideal is to combine them, we find that there is a tendency for one to be lost as we try to provide the other. At certain points during the design process, it can be helpful to ask oneself how much harmony, how much vitality, is desirable in this particular scheme, and then what are the Function/ Stability requirements which will influence these aspects.

A critical factor in the development of a visual design is the matter of judging what we see — the sketches or diagrams we produce to describe the building to ourselves. In many cases we are using very limited infor-mation, line diagrams and thumb nail sketches to represent a wide range of colours, tones, textures, etc. Because we respond directly to what we see we tend to judge the sketch as a composition in itself. So, a good sketch will encourage us to pursue a particular idea perhaps to find that, when drawn to scale, the direction, proportions or solid-to-void relationships change to a point where our composition loses much of its value. Equally we can produce bad sketches of what might be potentially good arrangements. This means that there is a strong case for being able to draw well — and quickly — but there is also a danger of producing well composed drawings of what could turn out to be poor buildings. Interpretation of our sketches is part of the skill of designing. The drawings we produce during the design process can become an integral part of that process. For this reason alone drawing skills — the ability to represent a building design quickly and easily — are essential to the designer. This means being able to think about and represent three-dimensional objects without difficulty. It means also relating the true elements of composition by means of drawing. For instance, a drawing which uses lines and tone only and suggests a satisfactory composition will eventually lead to a building with many more elements, and thus a danger of too many interests. The bold simplicity of a black and white sketch may be lost in the range of building materials which are likely to occur in the finished work.

At some stage in the design process, and preferably early, drawings must allow us to judge the visual effect of the materials to be used. Thus, the total

15

design process cannot be restricted to work in the drawing office. Reference to samples of materials and the experience of seeing the final effect of our design in finished buildings all have a part to play in developing design skill. Because our drawings may show only a few of the elements of a composition they can often give a false impression of lacking vitality. A drawing indicating tone and direction may not convey the effect of colour or texture. The consequence of this is that the final building will have more elements and more interest than the drawings suggest. For this reason, the drawings should give a sense of bold simplicity and we must avoid the temptation to go on adding contrasts to a design or the finished result will be in danger of becoming fussy, lacking clarity and producing a multiplicity of competing interests which destroy the unity we saw in the drawings.

We will be looking at the wider setting of a design as part of the principle of Magnitude. The site, although outside the building, is still under our sphere of influence and should be considered as part of the total visual composition. Paths, terraces and paving, particularly planting, are all visual elements to be related to the building.

Landscape architecture needs special knowledge: here the elements of composition are constantly changing with the seasons and growth. I think that all architects should have at least a basic understanding of landscape work, if only to realise when expert advice is needed. The arrangement of external elements near to the building have a particular relevance to the total visual design. The simple forms and bold massing of modern architecture can be softened by planting. The natural elements can also give subtle contrast to the building forms. Heavy landscaping can be used for functional purposes as well and the effect upon light and sound may be of particular importance to the building design. The overall relationship between building and site can provide as much vitality — for instance — as the contrasts within the building composition. Japanese architecture, like the traditional English country house, combines formal buildings with informal settings. The small French towns with their squares full of trees and the tree-lined boulevards of the cities combine shade with a pleasant contrast between buildings and foliage.

The relationship between solid and void is a very strong element of external composition. In normal circumstances, the voids — openings or windows — appear dark and so tend to provide tonal contrast as well. Openings can give directional emphasis at the same time as providing a basis for proportional arrangements. Traditional styles of architecture employed strict control of openings which, with decoration, gave formal emphasis and rhythms.

Group of garages, Tapiola, near Helsinki, Finland
This is an interesting example of diminishing the visual impact of a group of garages near to and part of a housing estate. By turning the garages inwards it reduces the amount of tarmac turning space — all cars must share the same space. It provides a visually simple external wall and tends to reduce the spread of noise. The use of landscape and planting softens the visual impact and unifies the group with its general setting, the Tapiola landscape.

16

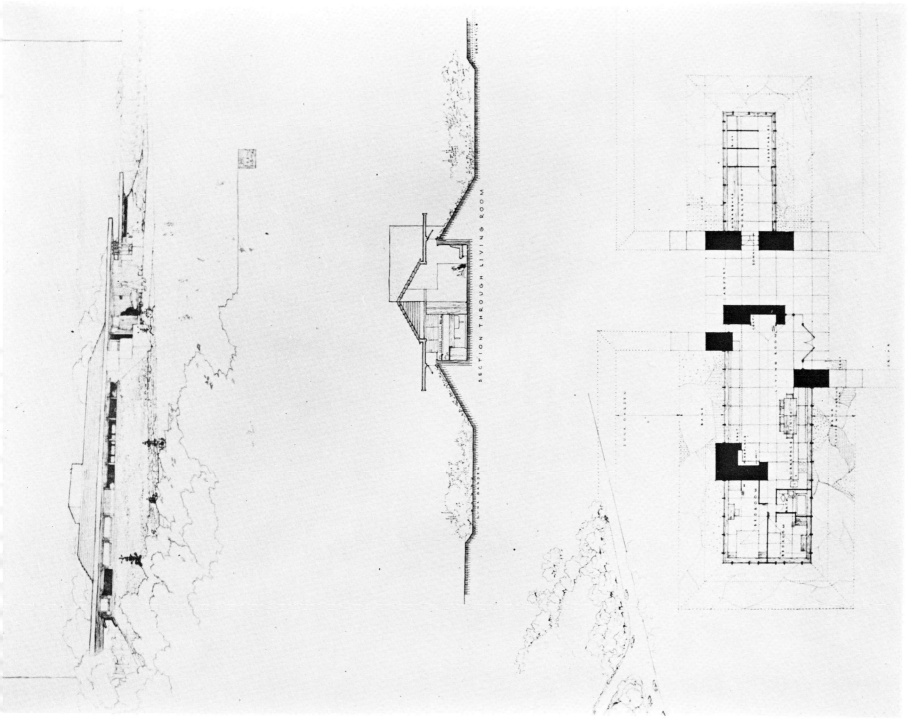

SECTION THROUGH LIVING ROOM

Berm Houses (Frank Lloyd Wright) for workers in Detroit, Mich., abandoned for lack of cooperation.
Setting the house down into the ground emphasises the horizontal proportions and the strong directional impact of the roof. Horizontal dominance.
© *Frank Lloyd Wright Foundation.*

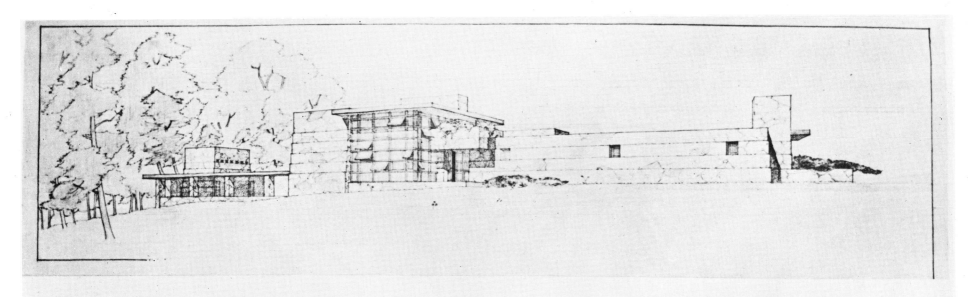

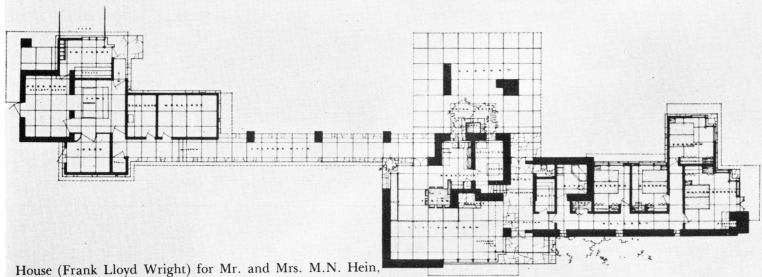

House (Frank Lloyd Wright) for Mr. and Mrs. M.N. Hein, Chippewa Falls, Wisc.

In the perspective view this illustrates a combination of contrast between horizontal and vertical elements. Note how the horizontals are emphasised by the set-back lines in the massive stone wall, while the verticals are relatively light, visually, in the columns and the large window where horizontals and verticals combine to give some verticality with stronger horizontal proportions. The solid-to-void relationship follows the same pattern with the solid predominant over the void. © Frank Lloyd Wright Foundation.

THIS house is entirely of native stone found in the countryside of Northern Wisconsin. It is the usual Usonian in plan but constructed with interior-insulated stone walls showing the same inside as outside. A semi-detached stable is a feature necessary to such houses in the country.

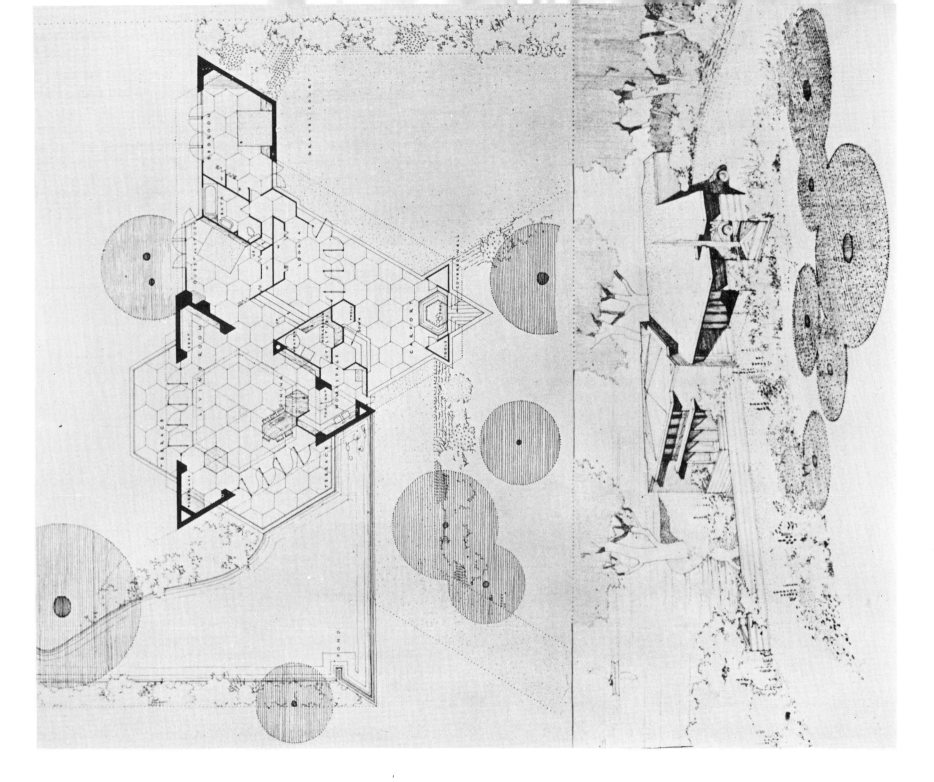

House (Frank Lloyd Wright) for Mr. and Mrs. Vigo Sundt, Madison, Wisc. An organic grid pattern of hexagons and triangles as a loose basis for planning layout and providing an overall theme. © Frank Lloyd Wright Foundation.

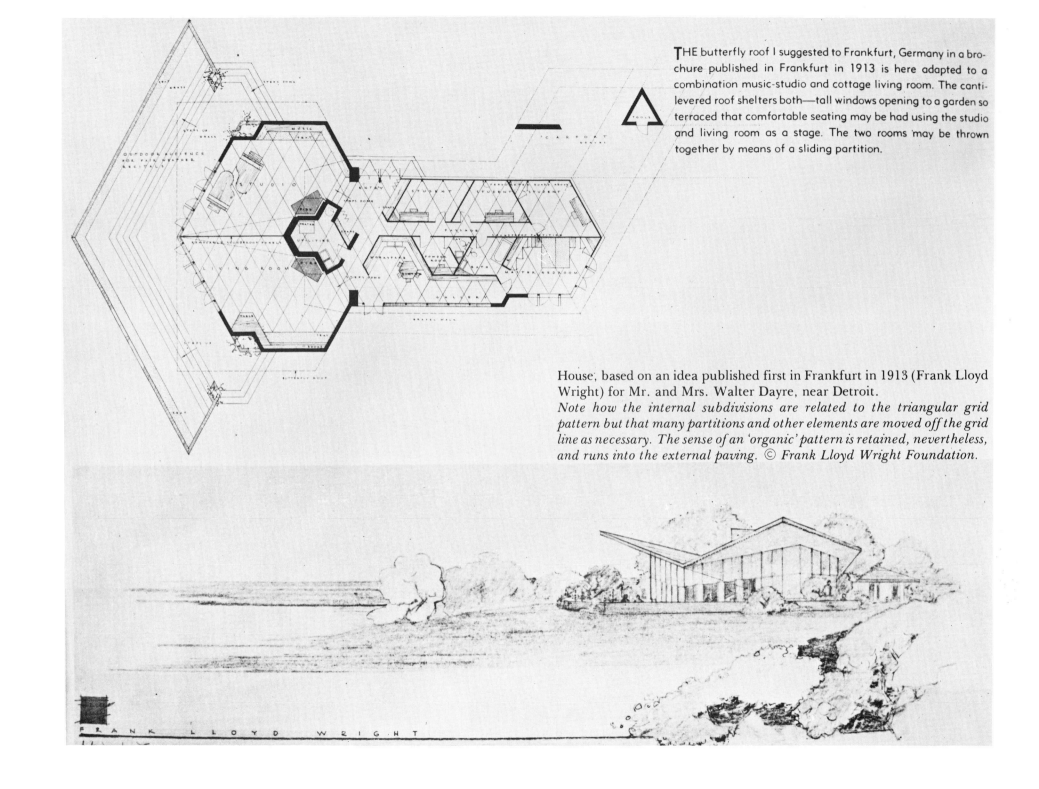

THE butterfly roof I suggested to Frankfurt, Germany in a brochure published in Frankfurt in 1913 is here adapted to a combination music-studio and cottage living room. The cantilevered roof shelters both—tall windows opening to a garden so terraced that comfortable seating may be had using the studio and living room as a stage. The two rooms may be thrown together by means of a sliding partition.

House, based on an idea published first in Frankfurt in 1913 (Frank Lloyd Wright) for Mr. and Mrs. Walter Dayre, near Detroit.
Note how the internal subdivisions are related to the triangular grid pattern but that many partitions and other elements are moved off the grid line as necessary. The sense of an 'organic' pattern is retained, nevertheless, and runs into the external paving. © *Frank Lloyd Wright Foundation.*

FRANK LLOYD WRIGHT

It is worth studying the effect of arrangements with strong dominance of solid over void, i.e. where the openings are very small relative to the wall and vice versa, where the building consists of an open framework supporting an upper structure or roof. Experiments with various combinations of openings in walls show how easy it is to recognise when a duality occurs; when the visual effect of solid and void seem to be about the same and result in a feeling of a lack of unity. Where dualities occur through equal massing of parts of the design it is possible to produce a dominant from one mass by reducing the visual force of the other. This may be done by breaking up the areas of wall or by introducing more visual elements in one part in order to emphasise the dominance of the other.

Examples are given to illustrate the visual elements and the ways in which the aspects of composition contribute towards unity. Because composition is a visual matter, it might be thought that its meaning is best conveyed by illustration. This is only partly so. While sketches can serve to show examples of elements and aspects of composition they do not determine the precise meaning or the difference between elements and the essentials of unity in the way that words can do. The important point for the student is to allow his own judgement of composition to emerge while attempting to recognise the meaning of the terms used. Most important of all is the ability to criticise and improve a composition by being able to recognise its weaknesses and make improvements by conscious decisions based upon that criticism.

In the introduction to the aspects of unity, I described simple designs as having self-unity. An extension of this quality can be seen in classical architecture where the symmetrical arrangement of the parts is such that nothing could be taken away — and little added — without destroying this symmetry and the unity of the composition.

Many examples include a dominant, dome, tower or central part, about which the subsections are arranged. This is usually an axial symmetry about one central line. Many Egyptian temples were extremely symmetrical in one direction, but lacked symmetry and even balance when seen from the side. Such buildings, by their very nature, seem inflexible and formal. Organic unity, by comparison, depends upon the repetition of smaller units in less formal manner. Gothic architecture with its repetitive bay structure gives a feeling of organic unity, although many cathedrals and churches do have strong axial lines.

Perhaps more for reasons of expression, formal architecture has been avoided in recent years. Nevertheless, there are cases where symmetry of layout can provide advantages. This is particularly so in large public buildings where it is somewhat easier to find one's way about when the layout is symmetrical. Organic design using geometric shapes such as hexagons and octagons are very popular with students. They enjoy a sense of being 'natural' by association with organic forms in nature. They produce dynamic plan layouts, repeated structural arrangement and aid the achieving of visual unity. Unfortunately, they also produce a number of problems which require considerable skill in handling. The thickness of materials makes the junctions between the 'cells' more difficult than in a real honeycomb, for instance. Roof drainage and top lighting can become a problem over a large area of such a building. The introduction of small spaces in plan may be difficult to relate to the organic grid. The Brussels Expo of 1958 saw two buildings using geometric bays in this way; the Spanish Pavilion with a system of independently supported 'umbrellas', and the Swiss Pavilion using flattened hexagons at varying heights.

The Canadian Habitat building by Moshe Safdie was a multi-storey organic form which suggested varied, but organic, human habitation. Large-scale organic developments of this kind have appeared as projects for 'plug-in cities of the future'. Cost and the reaction against large concentrations of dwellings has meant that such ideas have not progressed beyond the concept stage. It would be unreasonable to stretch too far the analogy between insects and people.

Frank Lloyd Wright favoured the use of organic planning grids as a design aid. He, of course, made the statement that the grid must be the servant and he the master. He didn't hesitate to move things off grid if it was sensible to do so. Geometric grids, like harmonic systems such as the Modulor, can help to provide constancy in design. They must be seen, though, as a means to an end — Unity — and not an end in themselves.

4
Expressiveness

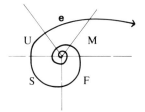

Our examination of the principle of Unity was concerned with the syntactics of design; that is, the visual relationship between each part and between each part and the whole composition. Our response to unity may produce a sense of pleasure or satisfaction when the composition itself is satisfying. However, apart from the visual order of a design, we respond to what we see according to previous influences or experience; the semantics of design — *expressiveness*.

To the extent which we share experiences, so we share the sense of expressiveness provided by a building. It must be accepted, of course, that each individual is unique and therefore will tend to differ in his response, depending upon the extent to which his background and experience differ from those of others.

In any group, society or culture, there is a large area of common influence. Each individual overlaps a major part of that common area, but may have some unique influences lying outside the normal or general experience.

Upbringing, religion, education, reading and television, provide many shared influences. Spheres of interest will occur at different levels also. We could say that there is a European background to the whole of western culture within which exists a number of national 'spheres'. Local and group influences occur through daily contacts with others, sometimes producing specialised or esoteric interests related to sport, work or intellectual pursuits. Our appreciation of the performance of a sportsman or a colleague at work is influenced by our knowledge of the subject and comparisons with the performance of others. Our conversation and behaviour within different groups varies according to the activity.

Our response to expressiveness may be partly subjective, particularly where early influences have become subconscious. Nevertheless, there are some aspects of expressiveness which we can examine objectively and I believe that any framework of architectural theory must include expressiveness as a principle, even if some of its influences are abstruse.

Because, when we look at a building, we respond to its composition and its expressiveness simultaneously, it is to be expected that the two effects are confused by most observers. For the student of architecture the understanding and control of composition often becomes possible only as a result of an appreciation of the differences between syntactics and semantics.

Poetry provides an illustration of the difference. The sound of words, the rhythm and rhyme — irrespective of meaning — provide a composition in sound. The meaning or expressiveness comes from the association which the words produce in our minds. The pleasure given by this combination of composition and meaning is much greater than the sum of the two parts. In other words, the evocation of a sympathetic understanding of the words is heightened by their arrangement in poetic form, and this applies whether we are hearing an epic or a limerick. When we see the architecture of an unfamiliar culture we are able to appreciate its unity, but not its expressiveness, unless we have studied the culture. So we may delight in the composition of the Ninomaru Palace Kyoto; its dominant roof and direction, its proportional harmony and contrasts in tone, texture and with its setting. Our appreciation of its expressiveness would be limited to its being Japanese, and not in any way the response of someone brought up in that culture.

Much of our response to expressiveness is determined by previous experience. We share a general acceptance of what is meant by a prison-like building or fairy tale castle architecture. School rooms and hospitals can have strong associations for most people and not only through vision. Sounds and particularly smells can be powerful reminders of the past. Religious architecture and the ceremonial of religion once provided a combined influence through all the senses.

The extent to which architecture is associated with pleasant or unpleasant experiences will influence our response to buildings that remind us of the past. Where buildings provide, or allow, or are even accidentally associated with, poor social conditions there will occur a reaction against the conditions — and the buildings. It is possible of course to have a happy childhood in a poor home and, less common perhaps, to have an unpleasant experience in an architectural masterpiece. So it can be that unity and expression may conflict. Early experience tends to be more enduring, probably because of the greater sensitivity and awareness of childhood. The depth of influence depends on the intensity and the duration of different experiences. Many people develop a 'blindness' to their surroundings — this seems to increase with its monotony and the extent to which the range of visual stimuli is limited. When we go abroad we are aware of strange surroundings much more than our normal zones of movement, but we take more notice of familiar things when we return — at least for a time.

Influences by association also occur in a direct way when a design suggests certain conditions by its appearance. A building on a heavily rusticated plinth or a wider base will imply heaviness, while an undercut base or under framing will suggest a lighter form. Roughness and smoothness of texture seem to have different weights, just as different colours may suggest variations in warmth. Windows glazed in line with the external face

Chateau at Azay le Rideaux, France
Fairy-tale-like romantic expressiveness, which most Europeans could recognise. The corner oriels and roof pinnacles against the setting of water and trees provide a dream-like quality much removed from the constraints of function or cost.

of a wall make the building appear lighter than fenestration that is heavily modelled and recessed. Sharp-edged oriels seem lighter than those with rounded corners. Many of our responses in this way are the result of early tactile experience. Thus, we know that wood is warmer than marble, that glass is thin and metal hard, all without needing to touch them. Dark shadows suggest bright sunshine (a point to remember in drawing designs).

Hotel Bavaria, Germany
An expressiveness associated with the Austrian Tyrol and southern Germany, given by the roof form and the painted gable. This is strengthened by the use of flower boxes (geraniums?), Gothic lettering and the details of wrought-iron lamp and the door construction. Note how the strong symmetry of the gable fenestration has been slightly offset by the position of the entrance: vitality through asymmetry in symmetry.

St. Anne's, Oxford (HKPA)
The crisp lines of the projecting window 'oriels' give a sense of lightness. The repetition and changes in this element and its proportions are important elements of a composition providing direction and vitality.

Office building, Stockholm, Sweden
The semicircular headed window glazing is brought out to the face of the brickwork giving an impression of lightness. The repetition and variation in form and position and the use of directional emphasis can also be seen.

Style and Fashion

Some aspects of expressiveness lie in the origins of a culture. Primitive designs embrace forms and patterns with mystical or religious meaning, such as the highly stylised and coloured masks and the building decorations in Papua New Guinea. These become associated with ritual to the point where, very often, the origins are forgotten.

As far as I know the Ancient Greeks made no reference to expressiveness in architecture. Yet the temples that remain were based upon early timber prototypes translated into stone and marble at the same time as being refined in composition. So the earlier origins were carried forward. In turn, Greek influence spread to Rome and thus through Romanesque, and later the Renaissance, to the whole of Western Europe and then throughout the world. Another influence, founded by Greek builders, started in Constantinople to become the Byzantine influence in Central Europe and the Middle East.

It is in this way that architectural styles are formed. *Style* may be considered as the collective characteristics of building where structure, unity and expressiveness are combined in an identifiable form related to a particular period or region, sometimes to an individual designer or school of design. In architecture the formation of a new style has usually been brought about by a few pioneers very often influenced by non-architectural thinking, such as the antiquarianism of the Renaissance and the literary Romanticism of the Revival period in English architecture. Those who followed the originators of a particular style were not mere copyists. Each style evolved to serve changing needs, to embrace new building techniques; and also to suit changes in climatic conditions as it spread to different regions. The style imposed a discipline within which the architects of the period worked.

An examination of Florentine Palaces, for instance, reveals the skill and versatility needed to combine the interior spaces into a complex, but visually coherent exterior, often on awkward and restricted sites. Renaissance pattern books were used by humble builders to produce Georgian domestic architecture and it was the discipline of the style which produced the civic unity of that period. The historic styles were visual and, although they evolved throughout each period, they retained a visual coherence. We can see Norman cathedrals, such as Gloucester, which have been 'improved' during the Perpendicular period and yet still remain a unified whole. Classical buildings of different ages exist side by side. They show their differences, but they are unified by a common style. The modern movement was not, at least in its origins, a visual style. The development of new materials and techniques and the emergence of new requirements, such as railway stations and factories, brought about a rejection of the older styles as unsuitable. 'Fitness for purpose' and 'Form follows function' became the slogans of a new movement which saw machine and mass production as the means of serving the rapidly changing and expanding needs of society. The pioneers of the modern movement produced work which expressed this spirit in the form of well unified compositions. The models they produced became the new style which, as in past periods, others followed. Unfortunately, the high rate of change in both needs and means requires a designer to respond to each problem afresh. Many designers do, but any unifying style, in the historic sense, becomes impossible. Lesser followers of the movement tended to do as their predecessors; that is, accept the visual forms of the pioneers. But if changes in building were rapid the spread of information about new work has been even faster and more widespread. The influences upon the architect have been enormous.

Rapid changes in method, and the growth of building engineering specialisations, have lead to an unprecedented increase in the need for technical knowledge and the application of building science. At the same time, the architect has been subjected to considerable influences in the form of visual information about buildings all over the world. It is easy to understand how we can find brise-soleil, which originated in hot climates, being used on European buildings. It may seem foolish, but it cannot be denied, that glass box buildings like the New York Lever have been copied elsewhere, but without the massive servicing systems which are obviously necessary for winter or summer comfort. Eclecticism, the copying of forms without proper consideration for their new context, has always existed. In many cases it was harmless; in some it even helped to provide urban unity which might otherwise have been unattainable. Eclecticism in today's conditions can be dangerous. Where visual influences are so varied it leads to a loss, not an improvement, in the unity of towns and cities. Where the influences of prevailing conditions are so wide ranging it can lead to unacceptable functional standards.

The cortile of the Renaissance palace was a haven of shade in Italy. It became a rather dark hole when transplanted to Northern Europe. However, it could be covered in, and artificial lighting has improved many a previously gloomy house. Society today expects higher and higher standards of comfort and safety. The architect must attempt to use new materials and methods to meet these expectations within strict cost limits.

Expression is no longer that of a style associated with gracious living or with spirituality. It is the expression of an age of rapid change, shifting values, high technology and competitiveness. It would seem, as always before, that architecture expresses the society which produces it. If we do not like the character of our present surroundings, it cannot be improved by a decision to do so superficially or by an Act of Parliament. The character of our towns and villages will change only as society itself is willing or able to change.

Fashion and style have similarities. Style tends to be used to describe longer and more clearly defined periods of architecture, while fashion has been associated with more transient influences.

In this sense, students have tended to be influenced by short-term fashions in architecture and even in methods of presentation. Sometimes a fashion will emerge in a school and fade after a time. Sometimes the work of an individual practitioner will become popular: I can think of James Stirling and 'Archigram' as having this kind of influence. In as much as this encourages a student to challenge existing attitudes, including his own, this is helpful; particularly when the student has to pursue the ramifications of a fashion to its ultimate details. The general effect of fashions is to foster a concern for visual objectives and that must be beneficial provided that function and stability are properly considered. The use of fashion as a visual crutch — an unseeing eclecticism or craze — can be damaging or dangerous. Thus with 'new brutalism' and 'neo liberty' there evolved fashions which could be said to have little to do with the essentials of architecture. This is a situation where architects form their own esoteric group which moves away from the expressiveness recognised by the whole of society to form its own 'in group', designing for each other and not for society as a whole. Such fashion is likely to enjoy popularity with designers because they need change, stimulus, vitality and new fashions provide this interest. For a new style to emerge, a much stronger movement must occur, involving all the principles of design and one which carries with it the will of society as a whole. Changes in architecture are more likely to be a slow evolution for some time until society can reaffirm its concern for what it builds as the setting for life; when the quality of life is related once again to the quality of architecture and the aims of society are towards improving the quality of life, in visual as much as in material terms.

Two recent styles should be mentioned, as I think that they still have some influence today. The De Stijl movement in Holland produced formal geometric architecture influenced by painters such as Mondrian and seen in Rietveld's houses in Utrecht. This geometric influence is perhaps best known in the work of W.M. Dudok. Another influence was pioneered by Ruskin and Wm. Morris in what can be called the 'arts and crafts' influence on architecture. This was examplified by Morris's own house at Bexley Heath designed by Philip Webb (1860). There followed the domestic architecture of C.F.A. Voysey and R. Norman Shaw. These English houses had an enormous influence upon European thinking and, through the book *Das Englische Haus* by H. Muthesius (1904), lead very indirectly to the development of the Bauhaus in Germany.

It is difficult to describe the impact that the new Bauhaus buildings had on young architects of the 1930s. Built by Gropius in 1926, it was a culmination of the twin effects of the geometry of de Stijl and the honesty of the arts and crafts movement, but accepting the machine now as an important influence in design. It came like a breath of fresh air in a Britain seen by its young designers as consisting of the remains of the Battle of the Styles surrounded by awful Victoriana. We may now see ourselves as surrounded by the wreckage of the international style, but the indirect influence of Mondrian and Morris can still be seen today.

View and Sunlight

The view out of a building and the sunlight which enters it have a major influence upon expressiveness.

Our response to a building will be affected by the prospect from its windows and by whether it receives sunlight or looks out upon a sunlit exterior. Windows may be introduced primarily as a means of admitting adequate daylight and may also serve to provide natural ventilation. Nevertheless, our appreciation of a house, for instance, will be affected by view or general outlook. Unfortunately, the view from our bedroom may be changed by development outside our control and there is no legal protection for a view. If the site is large enough, the outlook and landscaping can be controlled and become a part of the total design, contributing to expressiveness and unity. Many Japanese buildings on quite restricted spaces employ planting to give an impression of depth and privacy of outlook. In Northern Europe the sun is welcomed, for most of the year at least, and we attempt to introduce sunlight into houses and schools as an essential requirement of the design. Postwar schools in Britain were designed so that classrooms had a southerly outlook wherever possible. This, combined with the requirements for daylight and economy, often produced the problem of excessive solar gain during summer periods. Compact planning, for economy, lead to the use of larger windows for the required minimum daylight, and thus, with windows facing the sun, overheating of teaching spaces. This is an example of the competing objectives which the architect must reconcile. The effect of sunlight can be enhanced by the way in which external spaces are arranged to reflect the sun. Sunlight caught by shrubs and walls can produce a pleasant outlook from a north-facing window. The same features produce shadows when seen to the south. The greatest need for penetration of sunlight occurs in spring and autumn. This can be achieved by arranging the building in relation to the lower angle of sunlight at the equinoxes.

Of course, I have described the Northern European attitude to sunlight. In hotter countries the objective might be to provide shade with foliage and water to give a 'cool' outlook. Similarly the detailed arrangement to control air movement through the building would be influenced by external temperature and humidity.

In essence, the requirements for light, temperature and air are functional objectives, but their overall influence is psychological as well as physiological and thus affects expressiveness to a considerable degree.

Recent changes introduced by new school building guidelines in England reduce the earlier emphasis upon the need for natural light and simply require some part of external walls to include windows, mainly to avoid a claustrophobic effect. If interest is adequate within a building, as in a theatre or cinema for instance, a view out is unnecessary. In normal circumstances of work, and over long periods of time, we need to relate to the outside if only to know what the weather is like. However, the provision of openings in the walls of a room can provide glimpses of other external activities and are an important extension of our immediate surroundings. The view through a window is a concentrated picture of the external setting of the building and, as such, conveys an image of that piece of the world in which we live or work.

Expression of Other Principles

Expressiveness includes, almost inevitably, the expression of other principles of design. *Stability* in particular has had an important influence on style. Many buildings express their structural system, and the synthesis of stability and unity is an important factor in any design. Some architects have believed that the structure of a building must always be expressed

even to the extent of having nothing disguising it. This would seem to be an extreme view. I think that false suggestions of structure should be avoided, i.e. load-bearing buildings which are arranged to look like framed and cladded buildings, and vice versa. However, I see no reason for any blatant exposure of structure so long as this is implied wherever it is appropriate. Breuer's Bijenkorf store in Rotterdam is clad in a skin of travertine. The ground floor fenestration exposes the frame at that level and, where a slot is cut in the cladding, for instance at the restaurant level, the columns of the structure are again exposed. This implies a frame quite adequately. Le Corbusier's Ronchamp chapel looks like a load-bearing building with very thick walls. In fact there are columns supporting the roof, which can just be seen between the top of the wall and the underside of the roof. This is enough to suggest the structure.

Stability includes the materials used in building and where, in the past, local materials have been used extensively these have provided an indigenous expressiveness for many districts. This aspect of expressiveness is also referred to under Magnitude, but it is often a major influence where — through a collective expressiveness — the materials, even the structural system of a new design, may be influenced by existing buildings.

Stability in general produces a fairly positive effect on the visual design. Its essential requirements provide the basic elements of composition and, while expressiveness may go far beyond the requirements of structure, we can expect, nevertheless, to find structure as an integral part of unity and expressiveness. The buildings of the Gothic period demonstrate this fusion of principles, and the development of that style was an evolution of structure and expression, providing an organic sense of unity.

St. Anne's, Oxford (HKPA)
The interior composition reflects the exterior arrangement and uses the structural system as an essential part of the visual unity.

School, Berne, Switzerland
This expression of the structural system is an inherent part of the visual composition. An interesting example, too, of the use of natural forms in contrast with the strict architectonic nature of the building.

Office building in old Bremen, Germany
This building combines many elements of visual composition while expressing, simultaneously, the indigenous structure/construction of the time when old Bremen was built. The semi-structural semi-decorative brickwork is combined with shutters, decorative tensile tie ends and small-pane fenestration to give directional emphasis, solid-to-void relationships, texture, colour, tone and a sense of quality.

Function, on the other hand, does not have a direct effect upon expressiveness in quite the same way. A fortress or a bridge indicate their function, but many activities in buildings require only the provision of suitable space.

An office block, an hotel or a hospital may be similar in size, form and fenestration. Even department stores and libraries may employ a similar amount of window and, being for human activities, there may be little difference between them. Quite often it is only the arrangement of ground floor detail which gives any indication of difference. Sometimes the purpose of a building is suggested more by its similarity with earlier examples of the same type.

Industrial buildings do have a recognisable expression, but this is unfortunately more associated with their untidiness than any direct indication of function. Chimneys, cooling towers and large buildings without windows will suggest heavy industry or machine sheds. Even so, machines require men or women to service or control them and so windows provided for human needs may not necessarily indicate the main functional purpose. The massing and size of a building will tend to give some general indication of purpose.

Window arrangements can give a clue to function. Continuous windows suggest large internal spaces and individual units, smaller rooms, but this is not always consistent. In domestic architecture the variations in room size and purpose lead us to expect variations in window arrangements. Indeed, if all the windows in a small house were the same size and equally spaced we might find it difficult to believe that they were houses at all. Where housing units are repeated in large groups the expression of the individual dwellings is recognisable from the way in which the groups of windows and doors repeat. Of course, unvarying repetition on a large scale tends to produce monotony (under Unity) and implies a standardisation of human behaviour under expressiveness. It is this expression of standardised people which offends many observers, apart from the social problems which may result from large numbers of people being grouped in this way. The reaction against large blocks of dwellings, particularly high rise, is based on the social problems arising from these conditions. Certainly any concentration of people which does not allow them to fulfil a reasonable way of life, or which ignores the needs of young people or mothers with small children, will be unacceptable. However, it must be said that tall buildings in themselves are not necessarily bad. It is possible to imagine blocks built to penthouse standards that would be quite satisfactory for people without small children. The problem becomes one of cost and quality. The undesir-

able expressiveness of many urban concentrations is produced by monotony, degraded visual surroundings and lack of reasonable standards. There are large concentrations of flats in Geneva which include underground car parks, landscaped and well planted sites, shops and kiosks in the ground floor spaces with large apartments above, each having a large 'outdoor room' or inset balcony. The quality of the building and the variety of the units provides pleasant civilised housing areas close to the city and the lake.

Function is an aspect of expressiveness which should always be considered, but may often be no more than implied. If the principle of Function is given proper consideration it will tend to express itself in the solution — not necessarily in the exterior of the building.

The slogan of 'Form follows function' was a little misguided even if it was a necessary expression of intent at the time. The sceptics have claimed — quite rightly — that 'Form follows form'.

Flats, Holmstrup Terrassehus, Aarhus, Denmark
Interesting horizontal dominant composition with cross-walls of structure and staircases forming vertical contrasts. These are for private letting and, due to so many of the completed first phase being unoccupied, it is unlikely that more than a small fraction of the original scheme will be built. A reaction by the Danes against large concentrations of people and vehicles?

Flats, Geneva, Switzerland
High concentrations of people but in good-quality buildings with proper regard to family needs, open space, planting and parking of vehicles.

Quality

Quality is an aspect of expressiveness which may sometimes be difficult to predict during the design process. It is partly a matter of cost but not entirely so. Materials that do not stand up to use and are easily degraded will soon give a sense of poor quality even if they are expensive. Weathering of buildings can also cause a rapid degradation in appearance, even giving the effect of a change in the total character of a building.

The detailing we do for a building and the materials we choose must last for a long time and suffer a lot of wear and weather. If we do not consider such factors in detail the quality of the building, and its expression, will suffer. Sometimes materials are used which degrade at different rates (painting, rendering, etc.) and where less durable materials are used because of cost it may be important for the building owners to be warned of costs of future maintenance or the consequence of not keeping finishes in good order. In many cases neglect or even deliberate damage will increase as degradation, through wear or weather, lowers the visual quality of buildings.

Extreme repetition of any form or building tends to produce monotony, as discussed under unity. When any design, no matter how good, is repeated extensively it produces an effect of debasing its value. The use of mass production applied to building introduces the risk of both monotony and a cheapening effect.

City Theatre, Helsinki, Finland: foyer (Timo Penttilä)
A sense of quality is achieved through the generous space which is needed to accommodate a very important social activity during the winter in Helsinki when people meet each other during the theatre intervals. This sense is much enhanced by the use of good-quality material and excellent design in the details, such as the suspended coat-hanging clusters in the cloakroom seen on the right and the use of faience and marble in the interior finishes.

Le Chateau de Saumur, France: interior
A very simple interior space with plain stone walls and tiled floor enriched with superb tapestries, carvings and furniture to give a feeling of great quality by relatively simple means.

Many mass-produced products, such as motor cars, are dispersed and so reduce this effect. When large-scale developments of housing or flats are built together without change or relief the combined effect of monotony and lack of individuality is undesirable, both as composition and as an expression of human needs and behaviour.

Although people may have much in common it is a normal human tendency to express our personality in our surroundings. Most people do this inside their homes, many do it to their standardised cars as well, but where housing accommodation lacks variety it is not a true expression of people. Many suburban housing areas were lacking in this way. Where there existed the possibility of introducing change through planting, this has done much to overcome the monotony as the trees and shrubs have matured. Parts of Letchworth and Welwyn Garden City now give the impression of a continuous garden with some houses and the variety of the natural forms obscures or relieves any monotony which existed in the buildings. Landscaping and planting can also be used as an aid to identifying different sections of similar residential areas. It is difficult to know what people really think about the character of their surroundings. While there is a shortage of housing the lack of choice prevents any true indication of preference.

In Cleveland, Ohio, a partial housing surplus had occurred. It was soon made clear that, while people liked their house to fit in with the general area and not be too ostentatious, they would not buy if the house was the same as the one next door and, even when the appearance was different, they did not want a layout the same as their neighbour's!

Conclusions

At an extreme, expressiveness can embrace all human culture, history and influence. The student of architecture would find it impossible to cover more than a small amount of the available material. As a basis the student should extend his spheres of interest as widely as possible and avoid too limited a concentration upon the practicalities of building. While a wide field of interest is desirable an enthusiasm for any hobby or sport can help to extend one's interests. Exposure to unfamiliar cultures is of great benefit to the student. It not only extends his knowledge, but tends to produce a better appreciation of his own culture, too often taken for granted.

Cathedral, Lubek, Germany: interior
This largely rebuilt cathedral has a stark white-painted interior with tastefully designed simple modern pews. The highly ornate screen and crucifix seen here convey a strong sense of European religious expression and this sense is continued and reinforced by many, relatively small, minor details.

It is perhaps paradoxical that expressiveness, which can be the most important principle of all, is best appreciated by the study of these things which many would consider to have little to do with architecture. We should ask ourselves, when designing any building, what should it express? Is it ourselves? (At one time it was a widely held view that architects built monuments to themselves.) Is it function or stability? How important are these in this particular design? Is it society as it exists or are we perhaps trying to produce a building which will be suitable for society 35 years ahead, the half life of the building? I suspect that many architects try to express in their buildings their own view of a little of the future. Of course this happens in some cases anyway, because the influential building helps to create the future as architecture evolves.

Architecture has always evolved, it is evolving now, and in the process it expresses our civilisation — or lack of it. Architecture is a mirror of society and it should help to influence and change us where we find ourselves wanting.

5
Magnitude

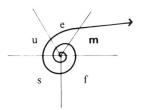

The principle of magnitude is concerned with major relative values. These values can influence our attitude to other principles and even override them in certain cases. The general aspects of magnitude are: first, the relationship between the design and man as an observer; second, the relationship to place; and, third, the relationship to time.

Scale

We compare everything we see to our own size. This is done instinctively and usually subconsciously. We are often only aware of this when we see again something, like a building or a garden, which we last saw in childhood. The place appears to have shrunk, but this is simply because we last compared it to our size as a child. We are accustomed to buildings being bigger than we are, but this is a relative judgement. When buildings or other objects are very big we are impressed by their size alone. Palaces were built big to be impressive. Temples and cathedrals suggest by their size that they serve something bigger, or more important, than man. Some buildings, such as railway stations and large machine halls, are big because of their purpose. More recently, we have seen a great increase in large buildings which are the result of the combined effect of structural possibility and high land values. Some of these have been made large for prestige purposes, where the name of the company is associated with the building, even when the company offices only occupy a part of the building. New tall buildings can be as exciting and impressive as any monumental building of the past, but when there are large concentrations of big buildings without relief they can become oppressive to the human scale. Open spaces and zones of low-rise buildings not only allow better penetration of sunlight, they can also provide spaces in which man can feel more in scale with his surroundings. Apart from any social problems, it would seem undesirable for man to live and work and spend all his time in surroundings that dwarf him.

The sense of *scale* and changes in height and space can play an important part in the provision of visual contrast, giving vitality to cities. Narrow spaces leading to open areas give vitality to cities like Florence and Rome, and the narrow streets of mediaeval Paris are in sharp contrast to the wide boulevards of Haussmann's 19th century improvements.

Setting

We judge the sense of scale directly when we live among buildings. When we are designing and using drawings to predict our work it is sometimes more difficult to assess relative scale. Steps and handrails relate very closely to human size, as do windows and doors, but these can be exaggerated as they have been in many deliberately monumental buildings. Some windows and doors relate to vehicle or other machine requirements. The scale of some buildings, like the Tennessee Valley Authority hydroelectric installations, may be so large as to make man seem like an alien creature. We find size generally impressive but, possibly because we are upright creatures, height seems to be more impressive than bulk. For instance, an obelisk is more impressive in an upright position than on its side.

The relationship between a design and its SETTING is most important. In designing any building we consider its composition as a total potential unity, but in fact every design must be seen in relation to a much wider setting. It may be surrounded by other buildings or form part of a continuous street frontage. Even in the countryside, the rural setting will probably be bigger, and more important, than the building we are putting into it. In some cases this aspect of magnitude may override all other considerations.

If part of the Circus in Bath were damaged we would not hesitate to renew the facade to match the existing in every detail. This is because we recognise that the visual unity of the whole is more important than its parts, and depends on the precise and constant repetition of subordinate

Fylingdales, Yorkshire, England
A cluster of early warning radar domes seen against the background of the moors.

Fylingdales, Yorkshire, England
One of the radar domes a little closer with the figure of a man a little left of centre. These pictures illustrate the effect of relative size in magnitude between design and setting and design and man.

elements. In other cases the influence may be different. Chipping Campden has a wide range of different building types, styles and forms. The mediaeval Grevel's house is not far from a large classical facade; different periods and changing needs have produced a variety of buildings within the street, but there is still unity. It does not depend on exact repetition in the way that the Circus does, but on a rough conformity to height and scale and a recognition of the space which is the high street. Indeed, the variety of building forms and styles gives interest and vitality while allowing the individual buildings to be more honest to their purpose and their period. It is sad to think that the public's attitude to modern architecture is such that we are no longer allowed the freedom that has obviously been given to all the builders in the past. This attitude is easy to understand when we see so many high streets spoiled by the introduction of shops which are obviously more concerned with projecting a national standard image than with respecting the existing surroundings.

It is this difficulty which has led to a widespread attitude of conservation at all cost. In fact we must, as a preliminary to any design, determine what provides unity in the existing setting and ensure in our own design that we do nothing to destroy that unity and everything possible to sustain and strengthen it. This is not necessarily achieved by using the same materials, or by building in a past style. There are some Devonshire villages where the unifying effect of the warm stone and the thatched roofs makes it difficult to see how one could do anything but use the same materials and forms. But even here it is relative, as we find the village churches have a different character or even use different materials. The church, in this case, is a foil — a contrasting element to the rest of the village. When building a cottage between cottages, we must respect the existing buildings to a much greater extent than if the new building is less closely associated with the existing ones and if the purpose is different. The Perpendicular improvements to the nave of the Norman Gloucester cathedral introduced major changes, but these were carried out with a confidence and conviction that seems to be lacking today. Perhaps the lesson is that the later Gothic builders were just as concerned with visual objectives as their predecessors, but that they also felt they had advanced and improved since Norman times.

Conservation must be considered when building amongst other buildings. Ideally, we should be able to assess and analyse the aspects and elements of unity in the existing buildings, in a way which will allow us to take a more purposeful approach to design under these circumstances. We may accept that, in some instances, the new should be different to, or in contrast with, the old; where the client, designer and authority understand and agree on the design strategy to be pursued.

In building away from other buildings we must consider this aspect of magnitude with just as much care. In many rural settings the countryside will be the dominant visual element in the composition. The building, even in sharp contrast to its setting, will be a subordinate — dominated — element, at least at a distance. In the Italian Dolomites there are lakeside kiosks of a rustic form which blend into the wooded setting so as to be unnoticeable except at close quarters. Again, the designer must assess the quality and compositional elements of the setting and relate his design to the wider 'design' to the best of his ability. This does not mean that different architects would choose the same solution, but taste and sensitivity combined with the architect's creativity should allow the provision of a range of suitable solutions.

In some instances, the setting may be within the control of the designer, where this is part of the building site. Here, the surroundings become part of a larger, three-dimensional problem which must relate to the spaces beyond. On large sites, the landscaping is not only a part of the total composition seen from outside, but provides the views from the building itself and so influences the design in two ways. The works of Humphrey Repton and Launcelot Brown were concerned with major alterations to landscape. The scale and boldness of Stourhead shows the importance once attached to this aspect of composition.

We have considered the relationship of the building to its setting. The same consideration can be applied to the spaces within any building and the contents of any single space. Some arts, like painting, are more or less instantaneous in their impact. Others, like music and drama, have a continuous time element. In other words, we start at the beginning and proceed to the end in a linear pattern relating each part to that which has gone before. In architecture, some parts are instantaneous and some have a time element, in that we pass from space to space. Further, there may be no simple linear pattern of movement, but rather a random arrangement of possible changes in position and a reversal of previous movement. This is a very exciting and dramatic quality of architecture. For the designer, it means that many spaces, which may be considered as individual unities, must also be seen as elements in a larger composition related through time and movement. As a simple example, adjacent spaces may be similar and harmonious, or in contrast, give a sense of change and vitality as one moves about the building or sees the spaces beyond from within. Finishes and furnishings within the spaces of a building are all elements of composition in the same way that the materials of the exterior may be arranged to give unity. Some architects believe that it is necessary to control all the building contents and even fix them in position to ensure a suitable and permanent unity of composition. This does not recognise the need for change both as a practical requirement and even as an ingredient of unity itself. We change the furniture arrangements and decorations in our homes, from time to time, because we need change — in time — particularly when we spend a lot of time in one place. In general, and particularly when furniture is selected without reference to the building interiors, there is the danger of too many competing elements being introduced into spaces, with a subsequent loss of unity and a tendency to visual chaos. Where the designer does not influence the choice of furnishings and fittings, there will be a temptation for him to provide more neutral backgrounds to tolerate a wider range of choice in the fittings. Sometimes, when the provision of furniture has been ignored, we see the designer providing all the interest and vitality in his design, only to be saddened by the experience of seeing it spoiled as more and more visual elements are introduced through furnishings.

Time

Time is the third aspect of magnitude and influences a design in two different ways. The intended duration of a building or any work will affect the way in which we attempt to provide unity. A short-term poster will tolerate vitality that in a permanent building could become tiresome. The relationship between harmony and vitality will be influenced by time in this way. Stability, particularly in terms of durability, will be influenced by this aspect, although it has always been a problem of designers to be able to make something sound enough for a limited time, but incapable of surviving longer. Many temporary buildings look temporary all their lives and often last longer than some permanent designs. Ideally, we can also expect more permanent buildings to have a common — collective — durability. All the materials used should endure well for the life of the building. This does not usually include services and equipment which, as we will discuss under function, can be expected to require renewal during the life of the building. Whenever possible, the building life should be reflected in the whole building so that short-term renewal, such as internal decoration, is reserved for spaces requiring some periodic change, and so that exterior surfaces weather and improve with age. This total ageing effect can be seen

in the great works of the past. It affects the visual composition and the expressiveness of the design.

Time has another aspect. Although there may be occasions when existing buildings exert a major influence, as in the example of the Circus, ideally every building should be a product of its own time. For the purpose of function and stability this is the only honest way of proceeding. The difficulty is that, all too often, buildings do not express their own time in quite the same way as in the past. The reason, I believe, is that too many recent buildings have failed to achieve acceptable standards of unity and expressiveness. Priorities are given to cost and utility; a general lack of understanding of the essentials of unity, expressiveness and magnitude have led to insensitive developments against which public and architects alike are reacting. It would seem that there has been a failure of modern architecture. I would prefer to call it a rejection of commercial building. There are, of course, many existing buildings which should be preserved. There are many which can be economically conserved and give years of useful life. However, we cannot afford to preserve everything and sensible conservation has its limits. In the end we must build anew. To then attempt to disguise new work is uneconomic and dishonest. What we must ensure is that our priorities, particularly in terms of visual objectives, are right in all new work. The large-scale renewal of many city centres appears to have lacked concern for visual criteria. The forms of earlier building groups and spaces, i.e. streets, squares, blocks, etc., which most people can recognise, have been swept away without new formal arrangements to take their place. Whole groups of new buildings, which should have been considered as single visual entities, have been built by different developers, often simultaneously, but completely lacking in overall unity.

So we see several buildings all using different forms, colours, tones and textures, often with each building using several materials, so that there is no dominant, no harmony, just visual chaos. In other cases, buildings having no visual relationship with one another have been forced to use similar materials or maintain standard heights where these do nothing to improve the overall composition, but merely induce a sense of monotony. Attempts to resolve visual problems by rules have not generally succeeded. Basic principles and sensitivity could help to establish overall objectives that would be accepted by different architects working within the same town or city.

The argument that buildings should express their own time is an important one. It suggests that buildings should use the new materials of that time as a means of honest expression. This is so, but it does not mean that the use of cheap materials or claddings, which will wear or weather badly, can be excused simply because they happen to be new. Honesty in this aspect of magnitude does not mean that the requirements of other principles can be ignored.

Any design must be seen in relation to the society and technology for which, and through which, it has been created. An architect has a responsibility to be aware of all potential materials and techniques appropriate to his purpose. Further, with the half-life of most buildings still some 35 years ahead, the architect is attempting to provide a design to serve quite a long way into the future. The more important buildings of a period require even more consideration in this respect. Nevertheless, the expression of present time must be made with due concern for the total lifetime of the building. A concern for 'todayness' can all too easily become an expression of a cheap and nasty tomorrow. Quality in design requires a proper appreciation for visual order, as well as the use of materials which will endure and improve. It is not an unreasonable argument to say that for an important building to last, to survive physical, chemical and frost damage, marble and granite or their equally durable modern counterparts may have to be used.

Magnitude, as a principle, means looking at all the other principles together with the wider setting of place and time and the relationship to man.

6
Function

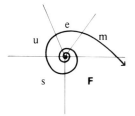

As applied to architecture, the term function has been used with a variety of meanings. In the early modern movement the pursuit of 'functionalism' was intended to combat the misuse of stylistic forms which were inappropriate to the purpose of the building. For some designers, the term has been used to embrace all aspects of architecture, including visual objectives. It really does not matter very much provided that all the objectives are recognised. It can be confusing, however, when there is more emphasis upon practical matters, and positively damaging to the student when he believes that a greater concentration on utilitarian objectives will produce a better total design. It has led, in some cases, to students believing that, provided the practical objectives are properly served, the visual result must be accepted as a natural by-product of the utilitarian design. It was because of confusions of this kind that the five principles of design were developed as a means of showing that, while all objectives are interrelated, there are a number of different objectives to be considered and that they can be in competition with one another.

For our purpose, let us agree that *function* will be used to describe only the basic practical needs the design must serve. In essence, these can be stated as *human, animal, plant* and *machine criteria*. Because buildings are fixed in their location and that location may be almost anywhere in the world, and because sites vary in the space they allow for building and in their contours and their services and access, we must consider the basic criteria as subject to *prevailing conditions*. It would be tedious and would not serve our purpose here to go into every aspect of function. We will consider the general framework and some aspects in order to illustrate the general meaning only.

Humans, animals, plants and machines form a vast field of study and the architect cannot possibly be expert in all aspects of physiology, biology, horticulture and the various branches of engineering. Yet a building which is to house any of these groups, and some buildings may serve more than one, must be designed with a reasonable knowledge of the essential functional requirements. When the purpose is very specialised, the architect must study these needs and will usually obtain expert advice — often through the client when the user is expert in the field. In designing for animals, the architect may have to undertake a detailed study of the subject in order to ensure that essential functional requirements are served. Of course, most buildings are for people and the natural assumption is that, being human ourselves, we are able to design such buildings from first-hand experience. This is only partly true: there can be misunderstandings about quite simple needs, and some human activities are specialised and cannot be considered as common knowledge. The experience of designing for animals can be a useful lesson to the architect, at least in appreciating how many human activities we take for granted.

Prevailing conditions can vary for every design. The same basic problem on two different sites will become two different problems when the site conditions vary. Differences in the shape of a site and the services and access to it can have the effect of requiring a totally different approach to the problem. An obvious example is where the site is spacious or restricted, resulting in a low or high rise building. In some cases the shape of the site or the adjoining property will affect the orientation of the building so that, even with a similar area of land to build on, the solution can be quite different. Climate is an extremely important condition: sunlight, temperature, humidity, rainfall, snow, frost and wind will be different from one part of the world to another and each has daily and seasonal variations for each location. An architect will normally operate within a particular region and, living in the area himself, will be aware of the range of climatic conditions affecting his buildings. When the location changes the prevailing conditions must be considered afresh. Even within a country as small as Britain there are considerable regional differences and a comparison between inland and coastal conditions may be surprising even over a short distance.

One very important consideration in the design of most buildings is the position of the sun. It is an important factor in the penetration of light into a building, in producing solar heat on and through the fabric and in the formation of shadows from surrounding buildings or the building being designed. Sunlight affects function and stability as well as having an important influence under the visual aspect of design. For example, in Bristol, England the sun rises and sets 40° North of East and West at midsummer and 40° South of East and West at midwinter. Its maximum angle above the horizontal is at midsummer 62° and at midwinter 15°. Such information together with daily and seasonal variations in intensity might be considered as part of an essential set of facts which the designer must have in mind while undertaking his design. Such conditions will influence the way in which the building is designed to serve the basic criteria. Apart from site and climate, there will be other factors which the architect must observe. Statutory requirements, for instance, are intended to cover many functional aspects. In most cases, however, they are not indicated in this way, but rather describe possible or mandatory arrangements (and so give solutions under stability rather than aspects of function. Nevertheless, Building Regulations are intended to enforce certain functional require-

ments. Some aspects of function are strongly influenced by social standards. Bathrooms and kitchens in Britain have changed tremendously since the second world war, simply as a result of changes in standards of living and developments in materials and manufacturing processes.

The full range of human activities extends from the cradle to the grave and embraces housing, education, work, leisure, medical and social services, including religion and recreation. All may require buildings of some kind. Within this range it is helpful to distinguish three broad categories which require different approaches to their design. First, domestic architecture: here we can usually assume that the users will take care of the building fabric and, as there are a limited number of people in a house, that sizes and finishes may be fairly modest. Second, public buildings: these are buildings for reasonably simple purposes but where, because of the use by larger numbers, will be subject to greater wear and damage. The third category we can call specialised buildings: these are where the activities are more complex and will require more detailed investigation as a preliminary to designing. Parts of hospitals, some industrial and manufacturing processes would be considered as specialised. Some buildings may, of course, combine public and specialised requirements.

In one sense, the category is influenced by experience and so, for a student, a house may require specialised study where the activities the building is to provide for are not fully understood.

Ideally, every design problem should be studied afresh as a preliminary to design. In practice, the experienced designer will need to spend less time on a subject with which he is familiar although, even so, it is dangerous to rely too heavily on previous experience as changes in standards as well as new methods and materials will eventually outdate previous examples. Changes in prevailing conditions can, of course, require radically different solutions.

Basic human criteria will influence all designs where people are involved. This may seem obvious but it is all too easy to reproduce previous solutions without reference to the essential bases.

Vision

The penetration of natural light into buildings was of great importance until 50 years ago. There were periods when safety was of even greater importance, and the effect can be seen in the fortified architecture of the

Middle Ages. Faced with a conflict of objectives, lighting had to give way to protection. The development of efficient artificial lighting had an enormous effect upon building design. Previously, for good natural lighting, a building's thickness was limited, particularly when internal divisions of space were required. Now, it is possible to provide adequate functional lighting by artificial means and so the thickness of a building is no longer limited for this reason. Hospitals and offices have been built with internal service 'cores' having no natural light. Depths of offices and schools have been increased using 'permanent supplementary artificial lighting' in the inner regions. Expressiveness requires a view out of work and living spaces and ventilation is a need normally served by windows in simple buildings. Windows can produce glare, solar heat gain in hot weather and heat loss in the winter; reasons for reducing their size compared with the over glazing of recent years.

A study of the development of post war schools in Britain shows the way in which the mandatory requirements for 2% daylight controlled building shape and fenestration. (2% daylight referred to a 'bright sky' norm of 500 lm, thus 2% = 10 lm. This would now read as approximately 100 lux.) The earlier standards for school premises were replaced in 1972 by Guidelines on Environmental Design in Educational Buildings, the latter allowing the use of permanent supplementary artificial lighting in teaching spaces and only requiring that a percentage of the outside wall shall be a window. This was introduced before the 'energy crisis' and it may be that artificial lighting may have to be limited to avoid unnecessary use of electricity. Against this, the smaller windows do permit better insulation, and heat losses in winter will need to be related to additional lighting costs throughout the year. The result of high energy cost, not only in school buildings, might well see a more careful arrangement of smaller window areas to give the best natural lighting and view out relative to maximum economic insulation of the whole building against heat loss. The recent reductions in U values required in domestic building are a foretaste of a trend that will affect all buildings. Traditionally, the arrangement of fenestration has played a major part in architectural composition. Some styles even suggest that the windows were arranged first to produce the required sense of visual order and the rooms arranged afterwards. The greater emphasis on function has overthrown this approach, sometimes with an obvious loss of visual order. Increasing concern for lighting and heat loss will provide a strong constraint upon fenestration. This does not mean, necessarily, that composition must suffer; perhaps rather that unity will be achieved through a more fundamental resolution of its aspects. The student must understand the functional requirements for vision, he must be able to organise his building in terms of natural and artificial lighting and attempt to co-ordinate them. He must not forget that light affects unity and expressiveness as well. The provision of artificial lighting on a purely functional basis can be monotonous and visually unpleasant. High-level high-intensity lighting over large areas of offices and workspaces is generally wasteful. Illumination for movement is required at a modest level, but lighting close to the task can be more effective and much more economical. In most cases the type and quality of lighting are more important objectives. The use of light fittings as decoration is largely misguided and produces strong visual elements which only compete with the other elements of the interior composition. While there is sometimes a real need for a decorative light fitting, too many are pretentious and little more than 'high-powered oil lamps' in the wrong place. Stage lighting is a useful study for the student who is interested in the scope of artificial lighting techniques.

Breathing

The human need for air must be considered in every building. Traditionally, it is provided by opening windows although a large quantity of air is taken in through the gaps around windows and doors. With the more careful sealing of gaps to prevent heat loss, the provision of controllable ventilation becomes more important. Wherever room sizes are small or occupancy high, the need for ventilation will increase. Consequently, the 'deeper' buildings resulting from new lighting methods also require more careful attention to ventilation and an increased use of artificial methods, in the form of either simple extraction units or more complex ducted air movement systems. Prevailing conditions play an important part in determining ventilation arrangements. In some countries the need for air movement may exceed the lighting requirements. Openings may be needed to give maximum air movement while restricting the entry of light and certainly the penetration of sunlight.

Hearing

While the eye is capable of adjusting quickly to changes in light intensity, the ear is much less able to respond to alteration in sound intensity. The prevention of unwanted sound and the sustaining or reinforcement of wanted sound are needs that the design of a building should attempt to satisfy as far as possible. The level of acceptable background noise depends on individual activities. The mind can tolerate and become accustomed to some levels of noise provided that the activity, such as reading or listening to speech or music, is not unduly interfered with. Toleration levels vary from place to place and at different times. A relatively unnoticed noise in a busy office in daytime may become unacceptable in the countryside, or at night when general noise levels are lower. There is an added irritation when one is unable to control noise from neighbouring occupancies.

Within any building or group, the activities can be categorised within a range of quiet to noisy and a design should be zoned as far as practicable to keep incompatible noise levels apart. Distance being a good attenuator of sound, zoning can provide noise separation fairly economically. Zoning must also take account of prevailing conditions, external noise from traffic and other buildings. Where distance cannot provide sufficient sound reduction it becomes necessary to introduce con-struction, to give sound insulation. Impact noise is best reduced at source by absorbent surfaces or mountings. The transmission of sound through the structural system can be minimised by breaks in the structure itself — not always compatible with the basic structural objectives. Airborne sound under most conditions is best reduced by heavy construction, mass being the simplest way of reducing sound transmission within the range of human hearing. Sound absorbent materials, which may reduce the reflection of sound within a space, may do little to prevent sound passing into an adjoining space. An open window or a curtain is very absorbent, but does nothing for the people on the other side. The English Building Regulations require between dwellings a reduction of sound ranging from 40 dB (decibels) at 100 hertz (cycles per second) to 56 dB at 3000 hertz. The designer must be aware of the value of the materials he uses in terms of their sound reduction value. For example, a concrete block or brickwall of 100 mm thickness may give 45 dB reduction while 200 mm may give only 50 dB. Glass, say 5 kgm^2 window glass, will give about 25 dB reduction. More important, perhaps, it is necessary for the designer to remain aware of the need for noise control and reduction against the spectrum of noise ranging from 30 phon in a quiet place to 130 phon at the threshold of painful sound.

In auditoria the main requirement is that people should be able to hear the speech or music, vision becoming important only when stage activities are to be seen. With small numbers of people in small rooms, or when the volume of sound can be increased, the fabric has only to absorb the sound that reaches it. In larger rooms it becomes necessary to reinforce the sound to the more distant parts of the auditorium. This is done by introducing reflective surfaces near to the sound source and possibly behind the distant seating. This has two effects: the reflective surfaces increase the reverber-ation time (the time from the sound being made to its complete decay) and sound is received via two paths, direct from source to listener and indirect via the reflective surfaces. Some reverberation time is tolerable, even advantageous, at about one second. This varies for speech and music and with the size of the auditorium. Big differences between direct and indirect paths can cause echo, and echo or unduly long reverberation time will confuse the sound received. Large churches and cathedrals are an exception in that church music has been developed to embrace the extended reverberation. Speech and other music may become unintell-igible.

A more detailed consideration, and I do not wish to become involved in too much detail here, is that the behaviour of materials in reflecting sound varies with frequency. If we check the probable reverberation times for a design we find that at, say, 125, 500 and 2000 hertz the absorption coeffi-cients of the lining materials — and the audience as well — will be different for the three frequencies and will therefore give different reverb-eration times for different frequencies. Generally, the more common materials absorb higher frequency sound more than lower frequencies. Thus, in order to produce something nearer the ideal, it may be necessary to introduce such finishes as lightly mounted polished panels which will, relatively, absorb more low-frequency and less high-frequency sound.

Apart from the functional aspects of hearing, the effect of sound and noise have strong psychological effects, which bear upon the expressiveness of a building. We 'read', from the way in which sound is absorbed or reverberates, the effect of space and finishes which influence our appreci-ation of the building. I remember visiting the British Pavilion during the 1958 Brussels Expo after the other buildings, in which people generally behaved as they do on holiday. The British Pavilion, with subdued lighting, had a high level of sound absorption with soft 'Pomp and Circumstance' music in the background. As people entered they put out their cigarettes, men took off their hats and everyone spoke in hushed voices. Control in reverberation from one space to another can provide interest under unity. We tend to become accustomed to levels of sound absorption/reverberation. Nevertheless, we are subconsciously aware of conditions, as we find when we move the furnishings out of a room we have been used to living in for some time.

Temperature

Body warmth, clothing and perspiration have modified the prevailing conditions of temperature to human needs for millions of years. Early buildings gave some additional protection against extremes of climate and the Minoan and Roman civilisation developed efficient systems using underfloor warm air by the hypocaust method. In this century we have seen tremendous advances in the means of heating, cooling and insulating buildings. Much of the development has been based on the use of cheap energy and we can expect further development to make better use of fuel and insulation. The advanced countries have come to expect efficient heating in all buildings, including housing, and even in vehicles. Dearer resources may necessitate a re-examination of the methods used in order to reduce waste. The basic requirement for human needs is to maintain a reasonable body temperature. Human temperature senses are such that cold surroundings will cause discomfort, and hot head and cold feet conditions are to be avoided. Close overhead heating or hot air directed upwards from walls is unpleasant and body radiation to surrounding cold surfaces can cause nausea.

The control of heating systems tends to be crude, resulting in discomfort and waste, such as when people have to open the windows of an overheated room. In cold weather, gentle radiant warmth with fresh air are ideal conditions, which are readily available but expensive. More economic and simple systems may be developed which will rely rather more on the use of natural body heat. One advantage would be that the body control mechanisms will be given greater use.

Cooling systems, although expensive to provide, can modify hot prevailing conditions. As with heating, over-provision is wasteful and can lead to excessive temperature changes, for instance when moving out of the building into external conditions. We should try to avoid the situation which has become quite common in many buildings today where energy is used causing overheating and more energy is required to cool the building.

Humidity

Humidity as a prevailing condition must be related to heating or cooling of buildings. Where humidity is excessive it will impose a further load on the building services and may require more specialised equipment and influence the overall heating/cooling installation.

Humidity can be produced by the activities within buildings, either by processes or through human activities and occupation. Apart from the undesirability of excessive humidity for human comfort, the fabric of a building may suffer as a result of condensation. Take the simple example of a bathroom. The water vapour produced can be ventilated, but will usually lead to a lowering of temperature in the room (in England anyway). Heat within the space can help to keep the moisture in a state of vapour, but condensation will occur when the vapour touches any materials with a temperature below the dew point. In excess this can damage finishes or be unsightly. When vapour condenses in porous materials it will reduce their insulation value and can cause decay or decomposition. Given warm conditions, low thermal capacity linings — which are not adversely affected by moisture — and gentle ventilation, the problem can be controlled. In less obvious activities the same process may be going on but more slowly. Vapour reaching porous insulating materials may cause damage and, where the moisture cannot 'breathe off', will lower the insulation value more or less permanently, thus increasing heating costs and leading to colder internal surface temperatures — and so steadily providing worse conditions. Temperature and humidity in this sense need to be understood by the designer and considered in relation to the thermal capacities of the materials of the building, their porosity and the provision of vapour and moisture barriers within the con-struction. Further difficulties can occur where moisture is present in the building materials and then subject to solar heat. This causes vaporisation, gas pressure and possible damage, particularly in roof finishes. Where timber reaches a moisture content above 20% due to condensation, and is untreated, dry rot, and even wet rot, can occur. Composition and fibrous insulating materials can become inefficient and break down under severe conditions.

Kitchens will produce both water and fat vapour. Surfaces that resist damage and are easily cleaned tend to have a low thermal capacity and thus precipitate condensation. At least it can be cleaned off. An example of vapour control in intensive cooking areas was given in a number of the Lyons quick-service restaurants, where they employed deep fat frying and grilling for speed of service. To reduce condensation, the cooking area was lined with stainless steel sheets (for ease of cleaning); these were heated behind (to reduce condensation) and the whole area was covered by a high-speed air extraction system (to remove the vapour).

Human Movement

Within a space or building, between spaces and from inside to outside, human movement is a major factor and influences the whole building arrangement. We talk of 'rooms' and 'circulation spaces' in building design, the rooms being arranged along 'zones of access' or 'corridors'. Vertical movement is an important aspect of design in a multi-storey building, for general movement and particularly for escape. Ramps, lifts and staircases relating one floor to another will have to be protected and well distributed when they serve as fire escapes. Movement, the space needed for activities, and the need for natural lighting, ventilation or view out are major determinants of building layout. Combination of low-rise and single-storey buildings employing roof lights can allow extensive continuous areas of building. High-rise buildings, with the restraints of structure and lighting tend to simpler and more limited plan shapes. The two forms can be combined in building complexes resulting in a cone-like formation which expresses human movement and lighting influences. Multiple high-rise buildings restrict cross movement; for instance, the problem of moving from top floor to top floor between the twin towers of the New York World Trade Center Building.

Height of building is limited by the speed of vertical travel, and cable weights limit the length of vertical travel in conventional lift systems. Acceleration and deceleration have limits for human comfort. Consequently, the time for moving up or down the separate stages increases to a point where height can isolate people from the ground level and external movement. Air or magnetically operated lifts without cables could reduce the travel time by allowing continuous movement through the full height of the building. Movement is not restricted to people: furniture and equipment may have a bigger influence in door, passage and lift sizes. A lift in a block of flats may be sized to take a stretcher or a coffin rather than for the number of people who will use it at any one time. Domestic stairs require more consideration for the movement of furniture than for individuals. Door widths must allow the passage of trays, trolleys and furniture even though one human being could probably pass through 350 mm. It is a pity that doors and passages in houses are not sized for wheelchairs and so give freedom to many people who are confined to one room or even obliged to live in hospitals simply because they cannot move about at home. Every design should be considered in terms of movement for disabled or wheelchair users. Many buildings must be designed for children or old people. In the home, children grow into the adult sizes of fittings and cope with stairs extremely well. Old people perhaps need more consideration; as their mobility declines the risk of serious injury increases.

The provisions for activities and movement are an important part of any design problem and yet, paradoxically, liable to considerable change during the life of the building. Certainly, one must study the initial requirements and the building must serve the purpose for which it is first built. Nevertheless, the activities will probably change many times and all buildings should attempt to allow as much flexibility of use as possible. In some industrial situations the processes may fix the method of working and the building design. In manufacturing, on the other hand, the need may be for a simple, uncluttered space in which machines can be operated. Here, even different activities are best housed in the same simple structure so that changes can be readily made and allow the use of a continuous standard building form. Clearly change is more easily introduced where there are fewer structural hindrances such as columns and large spaces, allowing a greater variety of use than small rooms.

Movement is required for people and for furniture and fittings, usually through the same passages, lifts, etc. In addition, a building can be considered as housing a number of different movement systems. Water, gas, air and electricity are the essential services, also materials and goods in the case of manufacturing processes. The more complex the services or processes the more care must be taken in integrating the different systems one to another and with the structural system of the building. In a sense one can consider a building combining different systems in one as being similar to the way in which a human body is a combination of skeleton (frame system) with lymph, blood, food, respiration and nervous systems all interrelated and supported in a single envelope.

Safety

The human requirements for safety cover a number of things.

Friction. The need for safety in movement becomes more critical where changes in level occur such as in staircases — even requiring additional safety provisions in the form of handrails.

Seeing. This becomes an essential part of safety in certain conditions and so natural, artificial and emergency lighting must be related to essential movement routes, particularly staircases and anywhere where a sudden loss of vision could be a hazard to safety.

Security. The prevention of unwanted intrusion can become a major factor in design. The castles of the Middle Ages were designed with security as the first priority. It has had much less influence in this century, but could become more important again if the present increase in crime continues. Roller shutters outside the windows of houses may have to be introduced on the pattern used in Italy for sunshading of habitable rooms. They can help to improve thermal insulation in cold weather too, like the combined windows and shutters used widely in Europe.

Fire. Protection from fire concerns first the occupants and second the building. For people, the important requirements are that the fire should not spread rapidly and that escape routes should allow them to reach a place of safety without having to pass through fire or smoke. The protection of the building concerns the choice of materials and the fire resistance of the structural system. Building Regulations, Fire Precautions and other Acts govern many of the provisions for safety, and Fire Officers give recommendations for all buildings. Many requirements are details which can be incorporated in the building design. However, the establishing of protected escape routes leading to a place of safety and within reach of all parts of the building is a matter of design strategy that can affect the overall solution and should be related to the provisions for movement generally. Security and fire escape provisions can be in conflict. They do need to be considered together, particularly as many fires are caused by intruders.

Nourishment, Hygiene and Sanitation

These could be considered as partly involved with movement and also with safety. They are essential to human needs and may have to be provided in any building.

Nourishment requires the provision of drinking water — in some countries this is taken to mean chilled drinking water — and food. Catering requires the supply and storage of food — in dry, cool or frozen storage — the preparation, cooking and serving of the food, the disposal of waste and the cleaning and storage of eating and cooking utensils. Food and eating habits are much influenced by established social behaviour, so cooking requirements vary from country to country and from culture to culture. Available supplies and facilities, even religion, can exert a considerable influence upon diet. Chilling, warming, boiling, baking, roasting, frying, grilling, steaming and preserving are some of the ways of preparing food. In a home the facilities may consist of an open fire or a single cooker. A normal domestic cooker can cope with most cooking requirements for a family. In a large restaurant or canteen the different processes may each warrant a separate piece of equipment. In very large kitchens the processing of pastry, fish and meat may be separated with different staff and equipment for each.

The by-products of smell, noise and rubbish mean that the siting and ventilation of kitchens require careful attention. The positioning of rubbish bays and the means of cleansing require an access point which will not normally be compatible with general access to the building, whether it be a house or an hotel.

Ventilation and hygiene in large kitchens constitute competing requirements which lead to the use of hard, easily cleanable surfaces, thus adding to another problem — noise, as the surfaces necessary to absorb sound are generally incompatible with the needs of hygiene. This means that care is needed in preventing noise in the kitchen from reaching the dining areas.

Sanitation and hygiene are factors affecting all buildings for human occupation. Some requirements for sanitary fittings are covered by statutory or advisory information from government agencies. Like kitchens, bathroom and toilet provisions have been subject rather more to the pressures of public opinion and advertising. Completely aseptic conditions are very difficult to provide, even in special areas of hospitals. The use of smooth easily cleanable materials looks hygienic and does aid cleaning but, nevertheless, staphylococcus bacteria can survive quite well in the joints between glazed wall tiles. Indeed, hospitals suffer from the problem of partial aseptic conditions where the balance of bacteria is upset and one type can increase to cause a more serious threat to humans than in the home. Where there is a balance between different harmful bacteria, human immunity is maintained by antibodies. European sanitary fittings have developed over many years and have been largely based on the use of ceramic materials, earthenware, vitreous china and fireclay. New materials have provided the possibility for new developments although most recent products still echo the more familiar traditional forms. Of course, human anthropometrics are an unchanging design factor. Where economies have been attempted by reducing size these have proved generally unsatisfactory: basins and baths need to be as large as possible compatible with water use and, in most cases, simplicity of form provides the most satisfactory visual and functionally efficient solutions. Large concentrations of people produce additional problems in the provision of toilets for schools or theatres. Generally, the use of dispersed smaller units of accomodation is better functionally, if more expensive, than centralised larger units. Again, the 'pressure of use' in public buildings places greater demands on fittings and finishes than in the home. Large units in constant use, as in motorway service stations, require an even higher standard of durability, better ventilation and much more supervision and maintenance.

The foregoing may serve to illustrate some of the human criteria which make up the functional requirements of buildings. It must not be forgotten that many buildings serve other needs as well. When buildings are intended primarily for animals or plants men will still need access for working. A small greenhouse takes its shape essentially from man's height. Many buildings for animals would be better and more easily kept warm if they were lower, but height and ventilation for man tends to dictate the form.

Machine criteria vary enormously. A nuclear power station is a giant machine with large building components directly related to the function of the machine. Every building contains equipment or materials in the service of man which, in turn, require servicing by man. The support, getting in and working accessibility of mechanical and electrical installations in buildings is now an important element in design and requires careful integration with the structural system and the construction of the building fabric. We have considered the need for changes in function in the general use of buildings. It is probable that the mechanical and electrical installations will require replacement three times in the life of a building, and other services, plumbing, drainage, etc. at least once. This means that services cannot be buried in the building fabric. Access for maintenance, painting or replacement is necessary, and the tendency of many students to put roof drainage pipes into the middle of structural columns or in the thickness of walls is misguided and leads to unnecessary complications in the erection and maintenance of the building. For this purpose, the architect must put himself in the position of the fitter with his wrench who has to erect or dismantle an installation. The organisation of ducts and pipes should be seen as systems related to the systems of structure and construction.

We have described the functional objectives as serving the needs of humans, animals, plants and machines in buildings. We must, of course, accept that the building fabric itself has need of protection from weather; sunlight affects the pigments of some materials; solar heat causes movement in many building materials; rain, in Britain particularly, is an ever present threat to the building fabric. Consequently, frost also becomes a threat to the building. Moisture movement of concrete and timber is caused by changes in humidity. Condensation affects unprotected porous insulating materials and can lead to rotting of untreated timber. Beetle infestation, chemical damage to stone and metals, rising damp and lightning are some of the prevailing conditions which affect the building more than its occupants and which can require special and sometimes expensive precautions. In some countries, climatic differences can alter the whole scale of prevailing conditions. The need to perspire, the threat of earth tremors and the threat from insects may replace the problems we have in dealing with buildings which are constantly freezing and thawing. The way in which we try to satisfy the needs of function may depend to a great extent upon the means available to serve them. It is easy to understand how needs and means become confused, how function — which is the objective — becomes inextricably interwoven with stability — the methods which we are able to apply.

It was for the purpose of improving understanding of this close relationship that the two separate principles were developed. It is helpful to look at them as separate groups of objectives; in the end, as with other principles of design, we must learn to see one set of intentions in the light of and through the limitations of another. All are inter-related, each can enrich the others; but while understanding requires analysis and separation, application and skill require a synthesis of all.

7 Stability

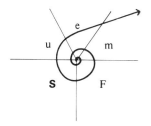

Stability is concerned with the materials and methods employed in the structure and fabric of the building; essentially the means of meeting the needs of Function.

The *structural system* of a design will be selected to meet the prime forces which will be imposed upon it, normally gravity and wind. The selection will be influenced by the ground conditions of the site and limited by the designer's range of experience and invention. Large-scale or complex structures may involve specialised knowledge and specialist engineers may be consulted. However, expert knowledge and experience is often achieved only at the expense of study in design as a whole. Any teamwork requires communication and understanding of the other members' work and therefore an architect should attempt to achieve an appreciation of as wide a range of structural systems as possible. This need not be limited to systems in common use, but could include a study of botanical and biological structure and extend into developments in other fields.

For a sound appreciation of structure it is necessary to understand the nature, potential and limitations of materials and their behaviour under stress. This in itself is a considerable task and one which has led even very good designers to work within a limited range of materials and techniques.

The stress exerted on a building is due to live loads (people, furniture, machinery, etc., not being part of the structure) and dead loads (the weight of the materials used in the building). The effect of these loads is to produce combinations of compression, tension, shear and bending stresses in the structure.

Certain functional requirements or limitations will tend to influence the choice of structural system more than others. In building, height, clear internal space, window or other openings, ground bearing capacity, fire risk, etc., will lead to the rejection of some systems in favour of others. Continuous vertical support, from external or internal walls to floors and roofs, is a traditional 'load-bearing' system widely used for small or medium-sized buildings where stone, brick or similar blocks are readily available. Timber, steel or concrete posts and beams, or posts and trusses, may be employed in a linear pattern, a grid form or as a three-dimensional frame. Arches, vaults and domes have been developed in brick, stone, concrete and other materials. Reinforced concrete and laminated timber have provided the means for new structural developments and no doubt metal alloys and plastics will permit further innovations.

In the past, designers were obliged to work within the limited range of structures available. Nevertheless, structural ingenuity and skill were developed, in some periods, to an outstanding degree. Gothic builders, limited to small stone units, produced complex arch and vault forms supported on slender piers, akin to a framed structure, to meet the requirements for large internal spaces and considerable window areas. Gothic building extended over some five centuries: it was influenced by Roman, Byzantine and Saracenic work and evolved and changed with time and in the process of transmission across Europe. Many structural systems are thus evolved rather than invented. Sometimes knowledge and skill are lost as a result of violent events: knowledge of Roman concrete and bronze making was lost during the Middle Ages, for example; medieval building skill was absent from the work of the Gothic Revival. In some cases, the potential influence of new materials is not realised by designers and, as during the early development of cast iron, steel and reinforced concrete, they were employed as a structural skeleton hidden by the trappings of other structural forms. There is an equal danger that new systems may be used simply because of their newness and novel appearance without regard for their suitability to functional requirements.

In machines and other designs, functional requirements such as mobility, portability, stress or flexibility, restrictions of space, support or fixing will tend to determine the type of structural system necessary. Frames, structural skins, monolithic forms or combinations of systems may be required. As in building, many systems have evolved over a considerable time. The arrangement of timbers in some traditional coachwork and farm carts shows how each member has been refined and shaped to produce the maximum resistance to stress for minimum weight.

The choice of structural system is largely influenced by a few of the functional requirements. *Con-struction* is concerned with the additions or modifications to the basic structural system necessary to satisfy all the detailed requirements. It is possible that constructional considerations may conflict with the structural system and some compromise may be necessary. Where a satisfactory compromise is difficult, this may be due to the structural system being unsuitable. For instance, the use of continuous load-bearing walls in buildings where the openings for windows, etc., can become so great that insufficient bearing area is left and the system is no longer suited to its purpose. To leave out columns halfway up a tall framed building to accommodate one large internal volume would complicate the system to such an extent that it would be better to consider placing the accommodation outside the general frame or, possibly, at the top of the building where columns might be left out without detriment to the system.

All functional requirements must be met by construction — resistance to climatic conditions, water penetration, sound and thermal insulation,

provision for movement, etc. — and, inevitably, there will be further competition between some of these provisions. The walls of a building may be part of the structural system in carrying loads for which compressive strength is needed; they may also provide thermal insulation, which is best given by porosity and lightness, and sound insulation, which needs density. These requirements may be satisfied by one material which serves all needs to a certain extent or by a composite arrangement where each material serves a different purpose. Just as the designer must familiarise himself with the various functional requirements, so he must study materials in order to understand their properties and the way in which they can serve these requirements. However, whereas it is possible to study needs as a preliminary to design, it is more difficult to absorb a satisfactory knowledge of structure or materials in a short time and it is necessary for a designer to have a comprehensive vocabulary of means. Too often a limited range of knowledge leads to the use of materials which, although familiar, are unsuited to the purpose. Too often even familiar materials are only partly understood or are used because they have been employed in broadly similar circumstances before.

Properties of materials should be considered in relation to the overall needs of function and at least a comparative set of performance values obtained for: strength in compression, tension, shear and bending, elasticity, mass, porosity, permeability, light reflection, sound reflection/absorption/reduction, thermal resistance/capacity/conductivity, resistance to fire and surface spread of flame, resistance to wear, slipping, abrasion, cleaning, etc. As there may well be several materials suitable for similar purposes, a comparative knowledge of cost is also needed as an aid to evaluation of cost-performance.

A most important part of construction is concerned with the making, mixing, placing or assembly of materials. A designer may not need to know how an alloy is made if he understands its properties, but he will need to know how it may be connected to other materials. The different ways of jointing timber or bonding stone or brick, the methods of forming concrete or plastics, all have a bearing upon the way in which materials may reasonably be employed in a design.

Many construction techniques require considerable skill acquired during years of training. While it may be an advantage for the designer to obtain this skill, it would be quite impossible to do so consistently where a number of skills are embraced by design. A pottery designer may need to understand all the intricacies of throwing pottery to enable him to develop the full potential of the material. Advantageous although it might be for a building designer to have all the skills of mason, plasterer, joiner and welder, quite obviously it would be difficult to master even one of these skills in addition to his own studies. The relationship between these skills, or crafts, and design should be understood. Because craftsmanship is difficult, concentration upon skill may exclude visual and even functional considerations. In learning to play a musical instrument, or to paint, one may easily become preoccupied with technique to the point where the composition and expression are ignored.

In a broader sense the total assembly of many designs is a skill which must, if understood, influence the designer. Building erection now embraces many new techniques which concern the design and which certainly affect the cost. This is another subject for detailed study but there are general implications which we should bear in mind. Early building techniques were developed within the limitations of manual labour with some mechanical assistance in hoisting materials, i.e. traditional craft methods. The same methods are still in general use, but the development of highly efficient and expensive site equipment, such as the tower crane, means that sensible economies can only be achieved if the equipment is fully employed during its period on site. This means that the weight of building elements must be related to the lifting capacity of machinery, all elements must have a similar weight and even the time required for machinery to hold the elements for fixing in position must be kept to a minimum. The basic cost of transporting, erecting and dismantling large cranes has tended to limit their use to buildings of fairly large size. A separate development has taken place in extending the scope of manual labour by a combination of lightweight elements and simple lifting and handling devices. Cladding of high buildings by the use of lightweight units fixed from inside can reduce plant costs where extensive scaffolding would otherwise be necessary. The importance of these considerations for the designer is in deciding, at a sufficiently early stage, upon the probable techniques of erection. This decision should then influence the arrangements for the structural system and general construction. The possible variations of structural system and construction present building designers, in particular, with so enormous a problem that there is an understandable tendency to employ 'stock' solutions, and sometimes these may be unrelated to the basic requirements. The acceptance of this attitude is shown in the widespread use of the term 'Design and Construction', implying the separation of the two. Design must embrace needs and means, but each should be examined with regard to function and stability in order to ensure that essentials are properly considered.

Building Regulations affect stability both in the structural system and construction. In general, most regulations are based on functional requirements and are intended to secure standards of performance where these are considered essential to public health and safety. Unfortunately, the need for legal drafting in statutes, combined with the concentration on control of method, disguises the functional objectives. The complexity of the regulations and the necessity for observing them, if work is to be permitted, may force designers to ignore the visual qualities of design and may even reduce consideration for basic criteria where it is assumed that regulations are bound to ensure adequate performance standards. As with the whole of stability, a designer must obtain a high level of understanding concerning the limitations of regulations and the variations possible within them. Basic understanding and experience can provide the versatility that allows a more balanced consideration for all principles.

What are sometimes referred to as the 'specialised requirements' in buildings, i.e. electrical and heating engineering, catering, lift and other equipment, have a functional basis, but have been regarded as special simply because they have involved specialised study or have become the work of consultants. The basic requirements have been referred to under the principle of function. The stability aspects of these subjects do involve specialised study but, as in the case of structural systems, the designer should attempt to obtain a broad appreciation of the limits and potentials of these fields. A general understanding of the principles of hydraulics, electricity, heating units and distribution systems, ventilation and other equipment, particularly with a view to controlling performance standards, is a necessary part of design training. However, the work in these subjects should not become isolated as, eventually, all must be integrated into the total design with due consideration for unity and expressiveness. Too many 'specialised' parts of buildings have been considered in isolation and designed as separate entities. This can lead to a mixture of arbitrary styling, making integration difficult and tending to destroy the total unity through a competition of many interests. Economic production may necessitate standardisation of many components or pieces of equipment, leaving the designer to select and integrate such items in his work. Where this must be so, there should be an appreciation of the principle of magnitude which could lead to a much greater simplicity in the visual organisation of components and a corresponding reduction in 'clutter'. Before the development of special equipment the architect integrated all practical requirements. For many years after the introduction of such equipment, buildings were designed as before and these special items added, very much in the way such services might be introduced into an old building. More recently, greater attention has been given to installations and attempts made to house services within the building fabric. While there is need to do so, nevertheless we must recognise that equipment is likely to change more rapidly than buildings and will probably need to be replaced more frequently. This being so, there is little advantage in the integration of services without proper access for repair or even complete replacement; it is more reasonable to provide clearly separated ducting and spaces which will allow for freedom of access and change without disruption of the general accommodation. If we may judge from developments in the more advanced technical fields, miniaturisation may tend to reduce the problem of integration of equipment, and increased efficiency could reduce the amount of equipment needed.

The experienced architect will have a broad appreciation of stability in which its aspects are seen as an inter-related whole. The student has the immense difficulty of attempting to design while his vocabulary of means is still very limited. This leads the student to work within a limited range of materials and techniques, and sometimes there is an understandable attempt to use new methods, but in a way which would be considered too great a risk in practice. It can be helpful for the student if stability is considered as its two main aspects; the structural system and the construction.

Every building and many component parts of buildings have an inherent structural system which should be clearly appreciated by the designer; even analysed as a special part of the design. The con-struction, the modifications or additions to the structural system, does require study and time in which to develop an adequate vocabulary. While the student is doing so it is important that the many materials and techniques are understood for their true purpose and properties and not acquired as a set of 'stock' solutions. In other words, stability, as with other principles, is a matter of understanding, and that understanding must not be neglected or allowed to diminish in the course of using constructional systems for different purposes.

8
Priorities

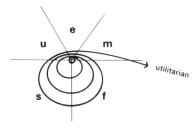

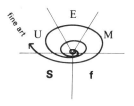

When we consider the number of objectives and the many competing requirements in design, it must be accepted, I think, that no work of architecture is going to be perfect. Compromise is inevitable and it follows therefore that the establishment and ordering of priorities has a very considerable influence. Even when we have determined our objectives and assessed their relative importance they will be subject to repeated re-evaluation during the design process. The way in which we work and the manner of preparing information for building purposes can introduce further influences which have the effect of changing the priorities.

Stability is important if for no other reason than that we cannot tolerate the possibility of our buildings falling down. The detailed drawings used for the construction of the building tend, of necessity, to concentrate upon the construction. This can lead to the heightening of the priorities associated with the principle of stability, visual objectives being ignored or forgotten. The basic functional objectives are closely associated with stability. The structural systems and construction are regarded as the means of serving the functional needs. Together, they may be considered as the utilitarian content of the design and, whatever our theoretical priorities may be, these basic practical requirements cannot be ignored.

Cost-performance or cost-effectiveness is the relationship between the design and the overall building cost. In theory, at least, there is no reason why good design should not be achieved economically. Indeed, the theoretical ideal is where unity and expressiveness are achieved through the essentials of function and stability. However, in practice, the importance of the utilitarian content of a design is such that, when cost is restricted, the priorities become weighted in favour of the practical necessities.

The public place a high value on the visual appearance of buildings and cities. The number of visitors to the historic buildings and towns of Europe demonstrate this as does the criticism of many recent buildings, thought of as modern architecture by most people. In this way, the public attitude to priorities is probably very similar to that held by most architects. The paying client, on the other hand, will be much more concerned with the cost of the building. Even when the client is a public body, the attitude to the spending of public money and the use of cost yardsticks, based upon the lowest costs for a particular building type, will give the greatest priority to the control of expenditure. Inevitably, this adjusts the priorities and the responsible architect must order his design priorities so that visual objectives become less important. If the client for the Cripps building at Cambridge states that he requires the building to last for 500 years, the architect can immediately assume that durability and visual standards are of a high order of priority. The general influence of building in Cambridge, near to fine historic architecture, reinforces the importance of the visual quality of the design. I am not suggesting that this makes the design easy; talent and imagination are still necessary, particularly to produce a good modern building in that situation. But only when the priorities are right is it possible for really good work to be produced. I believe that, given the right priorities, there is adequate talent in Britain to raise the visual standard of design to a level which would more than satisfy public opinion. Ironically, it is not only the public which has suffered from the lowering of design standards, but the profession of architecture itself. This raises an interesting dilemma: should the architect apply different priorities from those given or at least implied by the client? Most architects attempt to achieve a satisfactory visual order in their design even when they know that the client would resent any expenditure in its pursuit. However, constantly rising building costs and shortage of time for the design process do affect the priorities to the point where this becomes increasingly difficult.

The design process itself is complex and when an architect is repeatedly working through this process, with all the emphasis upon the utilitarian objectives, it can become very difficult for him to change his method of working even when the priorities are changed in favour of the visual objectives. The artist's objectives are primarily towards unity and expressiveness. The constraints of function and stability are of a low order and relatively easy to deal with. It is significant that, in periods of high architectural achievement, the architect was either an artist or closely associated with the arts or crafts.

The increased technical content of buildings today has two effects; the need for the architect to keep abreast of technical development and the greater complexity in structural, mechanical and electrical content in building inevitably affects his priorities. At the same time, for most larger buildings, the engineering content has become the province of the structural and services engineering consultant. Now this might be considered as an advantage whereby the architect can be relieved of the need to deal with the more detailed technical matters and concentrate upon the visual objectives. In fact, if a building is to be architecture there must be a synthesis of all objectives. This is unlikely to occur where the architect designs the building for the structural engineer to make stable and the service engineer to fit in his heating and other systems. It is equally unacceptable for the architect to simply clad the engineering solutions.

The answer must be either for the architect to control the whole design with the engineer simply checking the details — this is in many ways the ideal, but requires of the architect skills and knowledge which are normally beyond the scope of one man — or for the architect and engineers to be capable of working as a fully integrated team, each understanding the problems, limitations and potential of the others, but where priorities can be agreed and individual problems subordinated where necessary to achieve the prime objectives. One reason why I say that the ideal is for the architect to control the total design is because design synthesis, which combines logic and intuition, is best done by a single brain. Another reason is that the architect is still responsible for the total work and tends to be looked upon by the engineers as the co-ordinator of the whole, including their contributions. The difficulty is for the architect to maintain adequate control in all but the most straightforward of building types, the tendency being to move to one or other of the situations described, where the architect and engineer work in isolation and one after the other. The relationship between architect and engineer is partly a matter of the detailed design process. The control of design priorities can, however, be influenced or lost by the way in which architect and specialist communicate. Take as an example the design of a large auditorium. The architect may produce an exciting visual and structural solution, but an acoustic expert may wish to change the size of the space and the materials in order to correct the acoustic characteristics. Such situations do occur and are resolved by compromise, often with acute misgivings.

The design priorities, and the conceptual designs, must be established and assessed by all the specialists working as a close-knit team. At this stage, the specialisations must be represented by the most skilled, experienced and imaginative, designers in their organisations. The architect will still tend to have a central role because of his responsibilities and because he will usually have to co-ordinate the work of specialists. The difficulty of working in this way is that we have come to respect the force of scientific argument, which can generally be supported by logical analysis. In the face of several such analyses, how does the architect maintain the force of argument for the visual objectives, particularly when he is accustomed to seeking these at an intuitive level? There is a tendency to think that the logical technical analysis cannot be altered without loss of performance or increased cost — and so the priorities are adjusted. In fact, engineers deal with many problems only by assuming absolute values for many things which are highly indeterminate. A good engineering consultant knows this and will demonstrate a degree of versatility which may surprise some architects. The less able will tend to work more strictly within the limits of previous experience — as though there were no other way. Certainly my experience is that engineers display a respect for the visual objectives and the design ability of architects which may, in some cases, imply a lower priority for their own work than is reasonable or justified.

Architects' and engineers' training is different and their approach to design may often seem incompatible. There is a need for closer liaison and even closer training but, in the end, the team as a whole must be able to understand the priorities and the architect must be prepared to argue for visual objectives with as much force as the specialist will for his. Progress in this direction has been made through the establishment of multi-disciplined practices embracing architects and engineers covering the whole building process. Some of the larger groups have been successful as demonstrated by the buildings they have designed and the priorities which these display. Such grouping must allow for satisfactory development and rapport among engineers of individual specialisations and this implies rather large numbers overall. Individuals can become isolated in their own specialisation. There is no reason why quite satisfactory teamwork cannot be achieved between the traditional and independent practices of architects and specialist consulting engineers, and good progress has been made as liaison has improved. However, there is the danger of the architect being put in the position of patron to the engineer and this can inhibit free expression of ideas. It often produces the situation of the architect doing his design first and the engineer working within arbitrary restrictions.

The quantity surveyor is a specialist of a kind. Although originally concerned with measuring and recording the materials determined by the architect, he has become more and more involved in the prediction and control of building cost to the point where some clients will first go to the quantity surveyor in the belief that this will produce a more economical building. Certainly the quantity surveyor is much more aware of detailed costing than most architects but, unless the priorities are very clearly defined, a quantity surveyor's answer to a problem of cost savings will be made without any reference to visual matters. Engineers prepare drawings and for no other reason than this there is a basic relationship between architect and engineer which can quickly develop to an appreciation of visual qualities. Quantity surveyors do not make drawings, although they measure from them. They tend to keep figures and use accounts. This can alienate the architect and quantity surveyor when it comes to arguing about objectives. For this reason alone, the quantity surveyor's education should be much more closely related to architecture in order to allow him to communicate about the whole range of priorities in design. If this

were possible the difficulties of relating cost-performance in building would not disappear, but at least the values of architecture might be given better consideration at a point where greater and greater power is being placed.

The principles of design were developed as an aid to teaching, but it would seem more and more necessary in practice today to define objectives for the purpose of communication between specialists and for establishing all priorities in planning. Even the individual architect needs to be able to remind himself of what he is trying to achieve and the use of coherent principles can be helpful in maintaining priorities as the design work proceeds.

In education it is impossible for the student to embrace all objectives at once. Each design exercise must give careful emphasis to certain limited objectives and it is helpful to the student if he knows what the priorities are for any programme. For example, most students are anxious to give high priority to visual objectives. This can lead to a situation where every solution he prepares is so imaginative and unusual that he loses all contact with reality or normal building structures or con-struction. We do not wish to inhibit imagination, but inventiveness without practical knowledge will be fruitless and so some programmes should be written to encourage imaginative solutions while others must embrace the development of more basic skills and knowledge.

The question of cost limitations can be very difficult in education. If strict cost control were applied to every problem, priorities would be distorted from the outset and inventiveness inhibited as a result. On the other hand, imagination untrammelled by economics will find little place in reality. Therefore, cost analysis and the study of building economics must be so introduced that the student is at least aware of the probable cost of his solutions and is, occasionally, made to give this a high priority. Education cannot ignore the realities of practical building but the architect cannot develop all his skills unless he is able to practice them with a proper balance of objectives. The dilemma for education is in judging whether the student's priorities should be influenced towards those which generally exist in practice or those which might be considered ideal. In other words, the raising of visual standards as the public might prefer.

Priorities must be considered in relation to the priorities of society and life as a whole. Taking Maslow (*Motivation and Personality*) as a reference, we might assume that service to the community and recognition by our fellows are important aspirations for most people. In this sense we might see the quality of life and the quality of architecture as being synonymous. This being so, economic values could change to the point where cost-performance might be seen in terms of visual quality rather than utilitarian, but that will be for society to decide.

The conflict between public and private priorities represents the dilemma of the architect in establishing his own objectives in his work. The example of Cambridge represents the influences of magnitude in this dilemma. Whenever the setting to a new building consists of architecture of a high order, this tends to shift the priorities towards better visual standards. There is also the question of conservation but, this apart, the existing general standards in architecture do have a major influence in determining the priorities in new work. No one would dream of putting a utilitarian office block among the streets of Bath or Oxford (?). The Royal College of Physicians and the Economist Building are modern, but of an architectural quality which suits their settings. In Scandinavia and Switzerland there has been a general acceptance of modern architecture, and design standards have been established which influence any new work. No matter what the client's priorities may be, the architect would feel morally and professionally obliged to keep his standards up to the existing 'datum'. In Britain, there are now many towns where this datum is very low. This reduces the good influence on the architect and leaves him in a position where it is more difficult for him to argue for maintaining standards. It is much more difficult to raise standards once they have fallen, and Britain is in a poor position compared with most of Europe. It requires a greater effort, and perhaps rather more expenditure, in raising the levels of architecture. This in turn depends on money being available to allow priorities to be changed. The process will be one of further evolution in which economic progress will play a major part. We may wish to live in beautiful surroundings, but the question may well be whether we can afford to do so. If, on the other hand, we are unsuccessful in exporting manufactured goods to achieve the necessary standards, it could be that tourism may become a major part of our economy: in which case we should consider investing in better standards of building immediately!

9
The Design Process

Each designer develops his own way of working and I would not suggest for a moment that there can be a standard design method. Nevertheless, it is evident that there are a number of essential stages in designing, the understanding of which can help the individual to develop his own approach.

The first stage is the establishing of what we consider the problem to be. The solution we produce, eventually, will depend on what we believe we are trying to solve. If our understanding of the problem is inadequate, the solution will be the poorer. The difficulty, in architecture in particular, is in assessing all the objectives of design. Let us call the first stage — the design analysis — P; the statement of the problem.

The next stage consists of producing one or more tentative solutions to the problem — S.

We then criticise the solution. In forming the criticism C, we will find that we are not only criticising the solution but, indirectly, we are saying that our original statement P was inadequate. This is because, at the criticism stage, we bring to bear more or different objectives than we have set out in the first place. If our design is criticised by others, we may find that they are applying further objectives or different priorities from our own.

We can summarise the process as: problem statement P1, tentative solution S1 and criticism C1. This leads to the restatement of the problem P2 and so S2 and C2. Then P3 — S3 — C3 and so on. With complex problems such as architecture, the process can go on as long as time will allow. Because the result will be a single solution to multiple, and sometimes irreconcilable, objectives we must accept that it cannot be perfect. As we progress through each cycle of P — S — C, the problem is changing and the information and objectives tend to increase. Thus, the spiral can be used to illustrate the process to indicate that our knowledge of the problem increases as we attempt solution after solution.

This is theoretically so but, in many cases, and particularly during a student's early development, we may find that knowledge is not increasing but rather that priorities are changing. Lack of knowledge, particularly in function and stability, can lead to these objectives being given more and more attention to the point where visual objectives are debased. Sometimes the reverse occurs and visual objectives are pursued without regard for practical considerations. While design ability depends on knowledge and understanding, it is a skill. Like all skills it requires constant practice over a long period. The range of knowledge and understanding the student needs takes time to acquire. Many of the early design exercises are undertaken without the necessary understanding. In fact, the attempt to solve the problem is very often the vehicle by which knowledge is gained. Even when we have achieved some skill and appreciate the problem we are attempting to solve, it is not possible to produce a complete solution all at once. Let us assume that we have been through the process of analysis, synthesis and examination; $P_n - S_n - C_n$ and decided that the concept produced is generally acceptable. The manufacturing and assembly of the building elements and components will require far more information than is contained in the initial design. Traditionally, the initial concept was called the sketch design and this was then translated into the building process information and called working drawings. This suggests that the transition from sketch design to working drawings is simply a matter of detail and the drawing of parts of the building to a larger scale. In the past when we were building in a traditional manner, with a highly skilled labour force, it was possible to build from working drawings which contained little more information than the sketch design. The details were conventions which were better understood by the craftsmen than the architect. Today, even when the materials and techniques are based upon the traditional forms and crafts, much more information is needed simply to co-ordinate the building work and to allow the prediction, measurement and ordering of the many materials and increasing number of factory-made components. The result is that the initial, tentative, solution remains tentative for a considerable time while the details of the design are investigated and co-ordinated. It is therefore more reasonable to use the terms 'conceptual design', to describe the sketch, and 'operational design', instead of working drawings. The conceptual arrangement is largely a statement of intent for the guidance of structural and service engineering consultants and for use in obtaining information from the many manufacturers and suppliers who will be involved in the work.

With experience, skill and good fortune, it is possible for an architect to produce a conceptual design which will require very little modification in the process of developing the detailed drawings and specifications of the operational design. In most cases there will be constant modification. Often the operational design will reveal problems that have not been considered at the earlier stage. The result of this process is for the concept to be changed in many ways, usually for practical purposes, before the operational design reaches the stage of being final working drawings. This happens in practice even when the design teams are experienced in the type of work and in working together. For the inexperienced student it is obvious that he is not in a position to predict the operational problems at the conceptual stage. The necessary contact with manufacturers and consulting engineers during the design process may also be impossible.

In terms of gaining total experience and skill in design it is essential that the student is involved in a considerable amount of operational design work. For him it may not necessarily lead to the production of complete working drawings, but it should enable him to develop his design so that he is at least aware of the major flaws in his concept. There is a great deal to be learned from the detailed development of the operational stage. Much skill can be developed in the course of solving the problems associated with individual components and their assembly and integration in the total design. Because most students are lacking in detailed knowledge and experience associated with the operational stage, there is a tendency, whenever they meet a detailed problem, to want to go back and change the concept to eliminate that particular problem. This throws up yet more difficulties, but there is a danger of students failing to get to grips with the operational design simply because they keep backing away from it. Paradoxically, competence at the conceptual stage is enhanced by experience in operational design.

Of course there is no strong dividing line between the conceptual and operational design stages. They do, however, represent an important division in the integration of design teams. For this purpose, one could consider the concept to be the design stage which, having been reached — and agreed — by architect and specialist consultants, represents a group of firm decisions about essential systems in the design. These are structural and services systems in the main, but movement, construction and other systems may be determined at this stage to allow the specialist to move on to detailed analysis as a preliminary to the preparation of building information. The more complex the building, the greater the number of specialists, the greater the need for an agreed conceptual stage. Otherwise, major changes introduced after this point by one member of the design team will lead to the work of others being frustrated. The economics of design work will not allow this kind of duplication of effort. The smooth working of the team will be destroyed if one member upsets the work of others. In this sense the operational stage may be considered as the work done by architect and specialists in the investigation of their own area of work, but within the framework of the basic concept.

The priorities at the conceptual stage may include a fair balance of visual objectives. The operational stage is, by its very nature, much more a development of stability: structural systems and construction. It is thus very easy to lose sight of the conceptual objectives during the operational process. For this reason, it is sometimes helpful to introduce yet another design phase, the geometric: the detailed visual inter-relationships between all the parts of the building as the operational stage develops.

The visual objectives should be kept in mind at all stages but, because of the inherent difficulties of design team working, there is an increasing need to consider detailed engineering decisions in geometric terms. A heating or a structural unit may be perfectly practical, in accordance with the conceptual intentions, and yet its visual relationship to other elements of composition may be quite terrible. Many of the consultant's preliminary operational drawings need to be considered by the architect in this respect, while they are still provisional and before they become tendering documents.

The completion of the operational design, or working drawings, is not the end of the architect's or consultant's task. If the design has been worked out thoroughly the building process is no more than the realisation of all that has been predicted. This is seldom so in practice. Changes due to material or manufacturing and supply problems may be unavoidable. The difficulties which occur because of lack of co-ordination are of particular concern to the designers. These may be due to a clash of details; that is, where one consultant's or specialist's drawings have not been properly integrated with all others. The other problem is where unexpected visual elements appear, owing to specialist requirements or changes, and which mar the unity or expressiveness of the design. Here, the training of engineers and architects needs to be much more closely related so that the possibility of this type of problem is at least understood by specialists and so that they will inform the architect when the visual design is likely to be affected.

The traditional engineering approach to some specialist aspects is troublesome in this respect. There is a tendency, particularly in mechanical and electrical engineering work, to leave certain design decisions to the contractors carrying out the work. When the work is hidden in ducts or service areas with plenty of room to spare, there is no problem. But when the details become part of, or affect, the visual arrangements this can cause serious difficulties which may be expensive to overcome.

The greatest need is for a closer integration of all objectives in design. With more people involved this means better communication. While the architect must be able to understand the specialist and integrate his work within the whole, the specialist must appreciate that there are objectives other than his own and that these can be influenced by decisions which he takes about his own subject. The design process is a synthesis of many objectives and everyone involved contributes to the total design. Each is capable of damaging the whole entity. Architecture is the complete design, not a specialisation among other specialisations.

Notre Dame du Haut, Ronchamp

Le Corbusier

So powerful is the visual impact of this building that one could be forgiven for overlooking its practical aspects. However it is, essentially, a simple pilgrimage church equipped for worship inside and out, but with the basic essentials of a church, e.g. altar, altar rails, pulpit and pews together with the necessities of enclosure, such as windows, walls, floor and roof, taken out of the realm of the commonplace and becoming parts of a complex sculpture.

The Unity of the building is easily seen. It is both simple and complex. Simple, at a distance, with powerful roof and massive walls (dominance of solid over void) giving a bold and simple image. The two elements curve at right angles to one another and contain contrasts of colour, tone and texture. More interest (vitality) is given by the three curved towers, sympathetic to the curved forms of the building but introducing verticality into an otherwise horizontal composition. Note how the junction between towers and walls is articulated to emphasise verticality, and how the towers are grouped to form the entrance. The fenestration and other elements such as steps and gargoyle form a complex geometry. The window slots through the south wall change in size and shape as they pass through the wall, the proportions of which appear to be harmoniously related by the Modulor.

The interior composition follows the abstract composition of the outside with familiar items of church furniture handled in unusual ways: the fall on the floor, the proportions of the paving units and the way in which the plinth base to the pews has been pushed out of line illustrates a powerful control of detail — even a wilfulness. There can be no doubt that we are in the presence of a master sculptor employing a simple building as his medium. The closer one looks the more interest there is to be found, a never-ending vitality which is not cluttered or fussy.

Expressiveness in church architecture often relies upon the use of well known and familiar forms long associated with churches. At Ronchamp, it is difficult to find reference to any past work and yet — and this is probably the greatest indication of Le Corbusier's genius — the atmosphere is reverent and spiritual.

The Function of the building, like its Unity, is self-evident. The structure is more subtly expressed. The massive appearance of roof and walls could easily suggest a heavy load-bearing system but, in fact, the roof is a hollow structure and supported partly on columns and partly on blocks at the top of the wall, thus giving a lightness, particularly inside, which adds to the sense of strangeness. It could be argued that the structure is not properly expressed, that much of the walling is redundant, but it is just this use of structure which shows Le Corbusier's mastery. The massiveness of roof and walls gives the major dominant under unity; the dominance of solid over void. It also provides a sense of durability and permanence — an important aspect of its expression — while using the plasticity of concrete in the sculpted forms. The use of concrete also has the effect of indicating, without ambiguity, the building's place in time. While the concrete could be said to be used uneconomically, i.e. it has not been reduced to its structural minimum, the building, with its floating roof, does not deny its structural system.

Alpine Church

A building in this setting must have magnitude as an important consideration, and with a background of high mountains any building must be bold and simple. This design could be criticised for being somewhat too fussy for its setting but against that must be set due consideration for the demands of function and stability.

Its composition is generally good, and materials are reasonably limited in number. The stone in the base and the texture and colour of the roof material are similar and these contrast with the smooth rendered walls of the upper church and the cloistered floor above the base.

The grouping of the upper roof and spire gives a faintly pyramidal form to the whole composition and is an aid to unity. The rhythm of the cloister arches and the general emphasis on horizontality gives harmony, while the contrast in the walling/roofing materials and the strong vertical emphasis of the spire give vitality. The expressiveness is given by associations we hold for the cloistered ambulatory and the upward emphasis of spire. The cruciform lightning conductor is an unnecessary statement in expression but probably very necessary for functional reasons in this location.

The function is not very strongly conveyed; it is conveyed perhaps more by its expression than by any particular element of building other than the cloister. The complications of the roof formation are unusual in a region where almost all roofs are in simple single or double slopes without valleys, as a trouble-free way of shedding the water from melting snow. The structural system is obvious with its simple load-bearing walls. The cloister arcade supporting the cloister roof is a pleasant variation giving interest in the composition without too radical a change in the structural system.

Pattyndenne Manor, Kent

15th Century

The roof is the principal dominant element in this composition, although the oversailing first floor, together with the roof, seem to produce a dominant storey + roof (cf. Katsura), particularly where there are a number of changes and variations at ground floor level. The dominant direction is horizontal, but with the timbering providing vertical contrast and rhythm. The ornamental panels give some contrast (of form) while retaining the black and white contrast of tone.

The window sizes vary, as befits the functional requirements of a dwelling, and so does their spacing, so that the building has a 'natural' appearance which in no way detracts from its composition. Once more the structural system/con-struction is employed to provide the essentials of unity.

Buildings of this kind are often thought of as a 'rural' style — even 'rustic' — but in fact the visual composition is quite sophisticated. Much of the building detail and people's dress of the Middle Ages and Tudor period was visually sophisticated in a way seldom seen today. Coats of arms, emblems, decoration and dress combined expressiveness with visual subtlety and sophistication; as this house would express the taste and opulence of its original owners.

Sainte Marie de la Tourette, near Lyon

Le Corbusier

The most exciting architecture often combines a sense of inevitability with breath-taking inventiveness. This could be said of the Friary of La Tourette, where the sloping ground would seem to provide a great difficulty for the designer. Le Corbusier has simply designed a U-shaped block to house the monks' quarters and closed the U with the chapel. Simple and logical, yet brilliant in the way in which the accommodation has been devised to occupy the space it requires over the slope, leaving the space not required, between the underside of the monks' accommodation and the ground, to be taken up by supporting columns. The general directional emphasis is horizontal; the building, the grouped monks' cells and lines of floor slabs. Contrast of direction is given by the supporting columns and the vertical concrete glazing bars to the instruction rooms. The repetition of these bars sets up a rhythm, but the spacing is varied (on the basis of the Modulor?) to provide interest. The massive solidity of the chapel block contrasts with the more open nature of the living accommodation. The shutter-faced finish of the *in situ* concrete contrasts with the exposed aggregate or perforated finish of the precast panels.

The structural system is obvious, the Function less so until seen internally. But note how the essential structural system and con-struction of the building is used to give force to the aspects of unity; rhythm, proportion, direction and texture in the exterior of the monks' cells projecting out to form a dominant element in three facades.

The interior of the chapel is a striking example of the control of natural lighting in the design of an interior space. All the external light penetrates indirectly through horizontal or vertical slits in the walls of the chapel or through the side chapels with their angled roof cylinders. Le Corbusier has used these as a means of 'selecting' external light and, combined with coloured glass, exercises remarkable control over the internal expressiveness. As at Ronchamp, there is a masterly control of the whole building fabric with utilitarian elements used boldly in the service of unity and expressiveness. Even where difficulties may have been encountered, and anyone with practical experience knows how often they do, they have been handled with a boldness and confidence which seems to turn a potential nuisance into an advantage — certainly in visual terms. Once again, the more one examines it the more examples of this mastery appear.

The roughness of finish of many parts of this building is very different from the general tendency of the Modern Movement to try to produce pristine surfaces and junctions, yet it is entirely appropriate for an order of monks. The scale of the building also helps in this respect, as does the setting, so that the building is seen against a broad background of nature, not always the case where the eclecticism inspired by this building has produced extreme and inappropriate brutalism in design.

Katsura Imperial Palace, Kyoto, Japan

17th Century, Kobori Enshu

This building of the Yedo period (Shoin style) is an outstanding example of the art of architecture. Its subtle unity of composition is completely integrated with the structural system/con-struction.

Considerable interest — vitality — is given by the relationship between the ordered repetitions of the building with its bold dominant of roof + first floor and the site, in which the informality of nature is epitomised in a very romantic fashion. The building composition is full of rhythms and counter-rhythms with structure and infill panels related harmoniously, yet having contrasts of tone and texture. The structural system is a simple timber frame with indigenous Japanese roof timbering supporting the thatch cover. The con-struction is deceptively simple in appearance, but is used to produce a highly sophisticated three-dimensional composition. Materials are used in a direct manner so that they appear to be simply expressed, without adornment or contrivance, yet the building is full of delightful harmonies and contrasts produced by the way in which these simple materials have been used. A remarkable example of how the requirements of one principle can be obtained through the essentials of another, without diminution of either.

There is little to be said about the function of the building except that it is interesting that the planning of the building is said to be based on the dimensions of the tatami, the floor mat, as a design module.

As I stated in Chapter 4, it is difficult for anyone brought up in the culture of Europe to appreciate art expressiveness from a remote civilisation, our conditioning and educational/religious experience does not equip us to do so. Nevertheless, we can appreciate its composition and, for the student developing his or her understanding of design influences, it may help to study examples where one group of objectives, or another, is wholly excluded. Just as design exercises which concentrate on a limited sphere of objectives can enhance understanding.

Carcassonne, France

13th Century Fortified Town

The functional requirement for safety became so strong in Europe at this time that we can see how one aspect of one principle can dominate all other requirements. To the European of today it appears as a romantic vestige of an age of chivalry. For the designers, it was the result of sheer necessity for survival.

The absence of any large openings, indeed of openings of any kind to a large degree, provides a very strong dominant of solid over void. The consistency of the outer stone walling is a further unifying element. Vitality is given by the contrast between the mass of walling and such openings that do occur and, to some extent, by the change of material, texture and colour, in the roofing. The crenellations have an ABCBA rhythm supported by the repetition of the chute openings beneath. Even under the pressure of dire necessity there are a number of such features which demonstrate a concern for visual order which cannot be attributed to accident. Due to the need for defence against mobile attackers, the walls embrace the whole town, thus forcing a total unity upon the planning.

Olympic Arena Courtyard, Tokyo

Kenzo Tange

This space is partly formed by, surrounded with and contains a series of abstract forms which have been generated by the practical requirements and the building structure. Once again (cf. Le Corbusier and Frank Lloyd Wright) inventiveness has been employed to produce boldly sculptural forms from the essential requirements of the building; seating and lighting shafts, the spiral roofing and the oversailing soffit of the arena building become parts of a giant abstraction.

The function and structure are relatively simple. For the courtyard, the horizontal cantilevered roof covering part of the space runs on beyond the end enclosing wall and suggests that, like the oversailing slope of the arena, the courtyard is formed by buildings with other purposes, which is, of course, true. The dominance of plain white paving is reminiscent of traditional Japanese courtyard design and contrasts with the geometric forms of the seating — which also provides an element of repetition — and the lighting shafts.

The sense of strength of control over the details of the building to transform them into elements of the visual composition is a sign of the competence and determination of the master designer.

While there can be no doubt about the mastery of the visual composition, the expressiveness is somewhat less clear. It owes something to conventional Japanese work and yet it makes no direct reference to traditional forms or materials. What it does express, through magnitude, is that it is of the late 20th century. It is probably the confident use of the structural cantilever, and also the materials used, that give it this feeling of modernity, but there is no doubt about its era. Under the same principle, it might be argued that the sense of permanence is less appropriate for an Olympics building but it is probable that the brief called for a long-term use, other than for the games.

Chapel to the President's Palace, Brasilia

Oscar Niemeyer

This striking chapel design is an example of bold, imaginative simplicity. Its relationship to its setting is one of contrast with the flat plane of the raised podium and with the generally flat surrounding landscape. It is also in contrast with the adjoining Presidential Palace; equally striking and imaginative, but larger and more complex than the chapel. The building has almost a self-unity because it is so simple and plain, but the use of the 'natural' spiral for the structure cum enclosure provides interest and thus vitality.

There is little in its appearance to suggest that it is a chapel, but the interior will convey this sense and so it will eventually transfer to the exterior, by association.

The integration of unity and stability helps to achieve its simplicity and the use of concrete, in a way which exploits its potential plasticity, places the building in time.

Royal Portal, Chartres Cathedral, France

12th Century

Sculpture and stained glass are two powerful means of expression in architecture. At Chartres, we can see outstanding examples of both; architecture as an embodiment of the immense religious fervour that existed in France at that time. Here, architecture is seen as a vessel of beauty. Each visit is a greatly moving spiritual experience.

Research carried out by a group of architects studying the building for some years shows that most dimensions, for example in the size of openings and the stepping of reveals, are related geometrically, the predominant ratio being that of $\sqrt{2}$ to $\sqrt{3}$ or 1.4:1.7.

The stained glass of the windows is superb. The sense of mystery of the interior combines with a very architectural sense of movement. The utilitarian functional requirements are almost incidental to the major concentration on expressiveness which, as in most Gothic architecture, is integrated with unity and stability so that all seem one. This kind of expressiveness is not just for the building or for the people of Chartres who built it. It is the spiritual expression of the whole of a civilisation, a single building representing the aspirations of an age and bringing together the best of the materials and skills available for the purpose.

Mémorial des Martyrs de la Déportation, Isle de la Cité, Paris

G.H. Pingusson

This memorial, just behind the Cathedral of Notre Dame in the point of the Island, is a modern tour de force in expressiveness. The architect has taken the theme of a prison, the steps down to it, the prison yard and the cells and, with extreme care in the use and finish of materials, has raised them to the level of great architecture. The associations provided by these forms, even the echoing footsteps in the yard, are all reminiscent of the prison life to which those it commemorates must have been subjected. Yet the delicacy and care with which the work has been executed, like fine sculpture, expresses care and respect, as shown in the texturing of the concrete walls, the care in laying out and finishing the granite pavings, and the iron grille barring the inmates from the Seine, which has become wrought-iron sculpture.

This is an outstanding example of the way in which simple materials can provide great dignity.

Compton Wynyates, Warwickshire

15th Century

The unity of the building is maintained by the predominant use of pink brickwork and the dominance of solid over void. Vitality is given by the variety in the size and position of the openings and by details such as the timbered gables and the chimney stacks. Due to the alterations and extensions which have been built over the years the feeling is one of organic unity rather than formal unity. Its informality helps to express its domestic nature. The straightforward use of materials and country craftmanship also gives it an unselfconscious and honest Expression. Its informality makes it at one with its setting, rather than a contrast standing out. It functions as well as any building of its period can be expected to for present-day purposes of living. The structural system of load-bearing solid walls is simple and straightforward, combining stability with enclosing envelope, and one which has a relatively high level of insulation and thermal capacity.

The overall effect is one of age and charm given by relatively simple means.

Temporary Toilets, Munich Olympics Buildings

This is an interesting example of the use of mass-produced components. The repetition of the large units suggests that each has been stamped out by a giant machine. In fact, they probably had to be laid up by hand in very carefully prepared formwork, but the idea is there and is similar to the ideas embraced by F.R.S. York's building set for the film *The Shape of Things to Come*, where a machine was seen plugging panels onto a large building framework.

The danger inherent in such repetition is loss of unity through monotony and it is interesting to see, in this example, how change is provided by the higher services and water storage unit and the designer's use of a 'pod' with one clerestory window instead of two, on the left. Given even small changes like this the repetition of the standard unit becomes acceptable as providing rhythm and harmony.

The arrangement also suggests an organic growth pattern rather than a single formal solution. However, the handling of rainwater is not clearly dealt with and, even a short time after erection, the outside faces were showing stains from weathering with streaks running down the face to each side of the windows where dirt from the window units had been concentrated in one line as it was washed off by rain. The temporary nature of the building was entirely suited to its use in association with the Games.

Holy Cross Chapel Crematorium, Turku, Finland

Pekka Pitkänen

This elegant building uses concrete to achieve a design that is very well suited to its purpose and displays a fine balance of objectives. The major effect under expressiveness is one of dignity. There are also secondary effects, such as the way in which each chapel is closely related to the external landscape by its glazing arrangements. The simplicity of the interior spaces is achieved by careful attention to detailing so that there is an absence of clutter or appendages due to afterthoughts. There is a remarkable limit to the number of materials used, which also aids this feeling.

The unity is also enhanced by the use of few materials. In the exterior, the dominant element is horizontality; there is a dominance of solid over void — just — and the predominant material is concrete. The horizontality is accentuated by the way in which roof elements have been articulated from the walls and allowed to sweep over them. Vitality is given by the contrast between solid and void and the few vertical elements, the major contrast being between the building and the landscape. Internally, the chapels are simple rectilinear spaces formed by massive concrete blocks with very small joints in the walling, so giving a sense of permanence, durability and dignity. The major internal contrasts are in lighting and between interior spaces and landscape. The beautifully detailed pews are very simple and contrast with the concrete walls by colour, texture and tone.

The function of the building, in basic terms, is a very simple one but the arrangement for the catafalque to move slowly down through the floor at the end of the service is simple and dignified. The 'working' part of the building at the lower level, which contains most of the functioning part, was equally well detailed and equipped so that all parts of the operation, even those behind the scenes, are carried out with tidyness and dignity.

The structural system, concrete block walls and lightweight roofing, is fully integrated with the unity and expressiveness of the design.

The principle of magnitude is well integrated through the use of concrete — as a material of its time and the sense of permanence and human scale slightly exaggerated as appropriate in a building of this purpose.

The BMW Building, Munich

This is an interesting example of dominant verticality with contrasting horizontals. Also interesting is the expression of the structure and service cores which is suggested by the protrusions at the top. The form of building with its curving plan shapes emphasises the verticality.

The horizontal banding of windows and spandrels sets up a number of repetitions, providing rhythms which could become monotonous were it not for the inset storey. The colour and texture of the building are additional unifying elements which also suggest mechanical engineering and so aid expression in a minor way. The unusual form gives it a uniqueness which is probably needed for the building to become a symbol of the company.

A bold and imaginative solution with a strong air of competence.

Reading List

Alexander, C., Ishikawa, S. and Silverstein, M.: *A Pattern Language which Generates Multi-Service Centers*

Alexander, Samuel: *Beauty and Other Forms of Value*

Beardsley, M.C.: *Aesthetics: Problems in the Philosophy of Criticism*

de Bono, Edward: *Use of Lateral Thinking*

de Bono, Edward: *The Mechanism of Mind*

Broadbent, G.: *Design in Architecture*

Brunius, T.: *Inspiration and Katharsis*

Burke, Edmund: *A Philosophical Enquiry into the Origin of our Ideas of the Sublime and the Beautiful* .

Chermeyeff and Alexander: *Community and Privacy*

Croce, B.: *Philosophy, Poetry, History: An Anthology of Essays by Benedetto Croce*, Trans. Cecil Sprigge

Eden, W.A.: *Architectural Tradition*

Homes for Today and Tomorrow, HMSO

Principles of Modern Building, HMSO

Joedicke, Jurgen: *Architecture Since 1945: Sources and Direction*

Kant, Immanuel: *The Critique of Judgement*, Trans. J.C. Meredity

Kepes, Gyorgy (Ed.): Vision and Value Series, *Architecture Since 1945*

Lethaby, W.R.: *Form in Civilisation*

Maslow, Abraham H.: *Motivation and Personality*

Norberg-Schultz, C.: *Intentions in Architecture*

Osborne, H.: *Aesthetics and Criticism*

Osborne, H.: *Theory of Beauty*

Popper, Karl: *Conjectures and Refutations in the Growth of Scientific Knowledge*

Popper, Karl: *Objective Knowledge: An Evolutionary Approach*

Popper, Karl: *The Logic of Scientific Discovery*

Read, Herbert: *Education Through Art*

Rowland, B.: *The Classical Tradition in Western Art*

Rosenthal, H. Werner: *Structure*

Schofield, P.H.: *Theory of Proportions in Architecture*

Scranton, R.L.: *Aesthetic Aspects of Ancient Art*

Sullivan, M.: *A Short History of Chinese Art*

Wittgenstein, L.: *Lectures and Conversations on Aesthetics, Psychology and Religious Belief*

Wittkower, Rudolph: *Architectural Principles in the Age of Humanism*

Index

Index of Designers